THE BIG BOOK OF

Mind-Bending

PUZZLES

Terry Stickels

Official **MENSA®**
Puzzle Book

STERLING PUBLISHING CO., INC.
New York

Library of Congress Cataloging-in-Publication Data Available

2 4 6 8 10 9 7 5 3 1

Published by Sterling Publishing Co., Inc.
387 Park Avenue South, New York, NY 10016
© 2006 by Terry Stickels
Portions of this book are extracted from the following
texts, previously published by Sterling Publishing Co., Inc.
and © 1994, 1998, 1999, and 2002 by Terry Stickels:
*Mind Workout Puzzles, Cunning Mind-Bending Puzzles,
Devious Mind-Bending Puzzles,* and *Mesmerizing Mind-
Bending Puzzles.*
Distributed in Canada by Sterling Publishing
c/o Canadian Manda Group, 165 Dufferin Street
Toronto, Ontario, Canada M6K 3H6
Distributed in the United Kingdom by GMC Distribution Services
Castle Place, 166 High Street, Lewes, East Sussex, England BN7 1XU
Distributed in Australia by Capricorn Link (Australia) Pty. Ltd.
P.O. Box 704, Windsor, NSW 2756, Australia

*Manufactured in the United States of America
All rights reserved*

Sterling ISBN 13: 978-1-4027-3255-3
ISBN 10: 1-4027-3255-4

For information about custom editions, special sales, premium and
corporate purchases, please contact Sterling Special Sales
Department at 800-805-5489 or specialsales@sterlingpub.com.

Contents

INTRODUCTION . . 5

PUZZLES 7

ANSWERS 231

INDEX 332

Introduction

This collection of puzzles comes from four previous books, with a sprinkling of new ones—all emphazizing the fun of thinking. You'll find everything from word to spatial/visual puzzles . . . from math to logic. I picked the puzzles I thought would offer you the best challenge and still put a smile on your face.

I took the mission seriously. There are puzzles for the neophyte and for the very best puzzle solvers. With ten different categories, no one will be shut out of enjoying his or her favorite puzzles.

Now, it's your turn. Approach this volume in any manner that is comfortable. Skip around if you like. After, all this whole effort is to entertain you.

Let me know what you think. Send me a note through my website at www.terrystickels.com.

Have fun.

—Terry Stickels

PUZZLES

1

For the uninitiated, the first three puzzles are called cryptarithms or, more precisely, alphametics. Puzzle creator J. A. H. Hunter coined the term *alphametic* to designate words that have meaning, rather than the random use of letters found in cryptarithms.

The object of this type of puzzle is to replace letters with digits. Each letter must represent the same digit, and no beginning letter of a word can be zero. If properly constructed, alphametics can be deduced logically.

In the first puzzle, my verbal arithmetic leaves something to be desired. Assign a number to each letter to correct my addition. Hint: Make a box or chart to consider the possibilities of different values.

$$
\begin{array}{r}
\text{ONE} \\
\text{ONE} \\
\text{ONE} \\
+\text{ONE} \\
\hline
\text{TEN}
\end{array}
$$

2

$$
\begin{array}{r}
\text{NOON} \\
\text{MOON} \\
+\text{SOON} \\
\hline
\text{JUNE}
\end{array}
$$

3

This third alphametic is more difficult than the first two, and there is more than one correct answer. Hint: create more than one chart of values.

THIS
IS
NOT
+WITH
_____
WHICH

 4

If B + P + F = 24, what are the values of Q and T? Hint: Consider whole numbers only.

A + B = Z
Z + P = T
T + A = F
F + S = Q
Q − T = 7

 5

Here is a cube presented from five different perspectives. One of the views is incorrect. Can you tell which one?

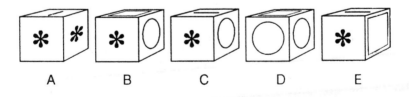

     A   B   C   D   E

6

Here is one way to unfold the cube in puzzle 5.

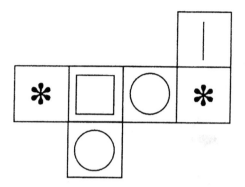

Here are two other ways to unfold a cube.

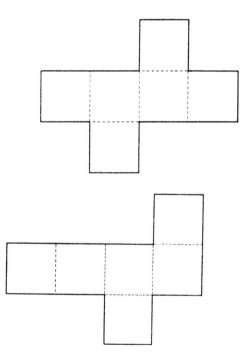

How many additional ways can a cube be unfolded?

7

Your boss has asked you to purchase three different types of ballpoint pen. The first costs 50¢, the second $5.50, and the third $9.50. He has given you $100 and told you to purchase 100 pens in any combination as long as you spend exactly $100 for 100 pens. Just one solution is possible. Can you find it? Hint: Familiarity with solving simultaneous equations would be helpful here.

8

Three of these five figures fit together to create a triangle. Which ones are they?

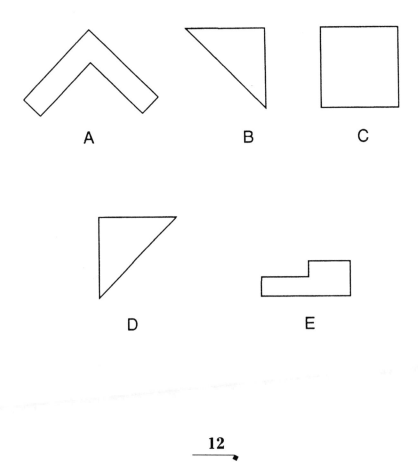

A

B

C

D

E

9

Here's a problem that will test your "layered thinking" ability. Give yourself about a minute to solve this puzzle.

Imagine that you have four kings and three queens from an ordinary deck of playing cards. (If you have access to a deck, the puzzle is more fun.)

The object of the game is to arrange the seven cards in an order that will result in an alternating pattern of K, Q, K, Q, K, Q, K. The seven cards must be held facedown. Move every other card, beginning with the first, to the bottom of the deck. Beginning with the second card, place every other card faceup on the table to reach the desired alternating pattern.

Remember, the first card goes to the bottom of the facedown pile, the second card goes faceup on the table, the third card goes to the bottom, the fourth card goes faceup, etc., until all seven are on the table.

What is the beginning arrangement of the cards?

 10

Mary has placed two chocolate cupcakes in one drawer of her kitchen. In another drawer, she has placed a chocolate and a vanilla cupcake; and in a third drawer, two vanilla cupcakes. Her brother knows the arrangement of the cupcakes, but doesn't know which drawers contain each arrangement.

Mary opens one of the drawers, pulls out a chocolate cupcake, and says to her brother, "If you can tell me what the chances are that the other cupcake in this drawer is chocolate, I'll let you have any cupcake you like."

What are the chances that the other cupcake is chocolate?

11

A team of cryptologists is in the process of developing a four-digit code that can never be broken. They know that if the code begins with 0, 5, or 7, it can be cracked. What is the greatest number of four-digit codes the team can use that won't be broken?

 12

Assuming that P, Q, and R have values other than those already used, what number, excluding 0, is it impossible for R to be?

$$\begin{array}{r} 2\ P\ 4 \\ Q\ 5 \\ +\ R\ 7 \\ \hline 4\ 0\ 7 \end{array}$$

13

If 7^{33} is divided by 10, what will the remainder be? You may get the wrong answer if you try to solve this on some calculators.

14

If the first three of the following statements are true, is the conclusion true or false?

All Nebraskans are Cornhusker fans.

Some Cornhusker fans are also Hawkeye fans.

Some Hawkeye fans are also Cyclone fans.

Therefore, some Nebraskans are Cyclone fans.

15

In a strange, distant land, they have a slightly different number system than ours. For instance, 4 × 6 = 30 and 4 × 7 = 34. Based on this, what is the value of 5 × 4 × 7 in this land? Hint: Remember this is a number *system*.

 16

Ann, Boobie, Cathy, and Dave are at their monthly business meeting. Their occupations are author, biologist, chemist, and doctor, but not necessarily in that order. Dave just told the biologist that Cathy was on her way with doughnuts. Ann is sitting across from the doctor and next to the chemist. The doctor was thinking that Boobie was a goofy name for parents to choose, but didn't say anything.

What is each person's occupation?

 17

See if you can establish a pattern to fill in the fourth grid in this sequence puzzle.

 18

The sum of the infinite series $\frac{1}{2} + \frac{1}{4} + \frac{1}{8} + \frac{1}{16} \ldots$ equals 1. What is the sum of the infinite series $\frac{1}{4} + \frac{1}{16} + \frac{1}{64} + \frac{1}{256} \ldots$?

19

This puzzle requires analytical reasoning. Determine the relationships between the figures and words to find two solutions.

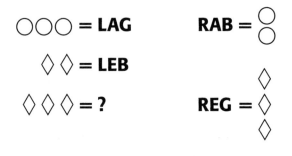

 = ?

REBRAG = ?

 20

Here's another opportunity to use analytical reasoning, but this puzzle has a slightly different twist.

In a foreign language:

"Kaf navcki roi" means "Take three pieces."

"Kir roi palt" means "Hide three coins."

"Inoti kaf kir" means "Cautiously take coins."

How would you say "Hide pieces cautiously" in this language?

 21

Seventy-eight percent of all people are gum chewers, and thirty-five percent of all people are under the age of fifteen. Given that a person has been selected at random, what is the probability that the person is not a gum chewer and above age fifteen?

22

What is the next letter in this series?

A   B   D   O   P   Q   _?_

 23

  A. 2^{65}

  B. $(2^{64} + 2^{63} + 2^{62} \ldots 2^2 + 2^1 + 2^0)$

In comparing the values of A and B, which of these statements is correct?

> B is 2^{64} larger than A.
> A is 2^{64} larger than B.
> A and B are equal.
> B is larger than A by 1.
> A is larger than B by 1.

 24

Classic puzzles are fun to revisit now and then, especially if there's a new twist.

In this puzzle, see if you can be as successful as John in retrieving water for his mother. The new twist? The buckets are different sizes.

John's mother told him to go to the river and bring back exactly 9 gallons of water in one trip. She gave him a six-gallon bucket and a five-gallon bucket to complete his task. Of course, John's mother told him she'd bake his favorite cake if he came back with the 9 gallons.

John had his cake and ate it, too. Can you?

25   **1881 : 1961 :: 6009 :   ?**

 26

In the world of physics, sometimes things that appear to move forward are actually moving backward. Knowing this, can you complete this analogy?

EMIT : STAR :: TIME :   ?

 27

What is the next number in this series?

1   9   18   25   27   21   ?

 28

Nine men and seven women pick as much corn in five days as seven men and eleven women pick in four days. Who are the better corn pickers and by how much?

 29

Puzzles 29 to 35 are all composed of numbers, but that doesn't necessarily mean that the numbers contained in any given problem are mathematically related. Your mind will have to be flexible to determine what type of relationship the numbers in the series have with each other. There are no holds barred, and each puzzle may have a solution more obvious than you realize at first.

What is the next number in this series?

1   2   4   13   31   112   ?

30

What is the next number in this series?

1   4   2   8   5   7   ?

Hint: This might be just a fraction of what you think.

 31

What is the missing number in this series?

9   3   15   7   12   ?   13   5   17   11

 32

What is the next number in this series?

0   2   4   6   8   12   12   20   16   ?

 33

What is the missing number in this series?

16   21   26   26   12   ?   19

 34

What is the next number in this series?

3   4   11   16   27   36   ?

 35

What is the next number in this series?

224   1   8   30   5   ?

No puzzle book would be complete without at least one anagram. Here is a phrase that, when unscrambled, spells the name of a famous person. The phrase gives a small hint relating to the person's identity.

BEEN IN STAR LITE

 37

Imagine a 3 × 3 × 3-inch opaque cube divided into twenty-seven 1-inch cubes. Quickly, what are the maximum number of 1-inch cubes that can be seen by one person from any point in space?

 38

What are the values of §, ⊗, and ¶?

$$§ + § + § + ⊗ = § + § + ⊗ + ⊗ + ⊗ = ¶ + ¶$$

$$¶ - § = 6$$

39

Below are four grids. See if you can determine the logic used in arriving at each successive grid. What would the next grid look like?

X	O	
O		O
X		

1

O	X	O
X		
O		

2

X	O	X
O		
	O	

3

O	X	
		X
	O	O

4

Bill is standing on the ground, looking directly at one of the faces of a new museum built in the shape of a four-sided pyramid. All the sides are identical.

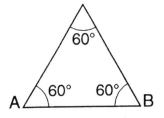

At night, each edge of the pyramid is illuminated with an array of colored lights. Bill's friend Judy is in an airplane touring the area. When her plane, which is several thousand feet high, flies directly over the top of the pyramid, Bill asks her, via walkie-talkie, if she can tell what angle lines A and B make at the peak of the pyramid. Judy answers without hesitation, but it's not what Bill expected. Why?

 41

Nitram Rendrag, the world's most renowned puzzle creator, often rents a private dining car on the Charlotte–Greensboro–Charlotte turn-around shuttle. The railroad charges Rendrag $120 for the trip. On a recent trip, the conductor informed Rendrag that there were two students at the Franklin station who wished to go from Franklin to Greensboro and back to Franklin. Franklin is halfway between Charlotte and Greensboro. Rendrag asked the conductor to let the students ride with him.

When the students boarded Rendrag's car, he said, "If you can tell me the mathematically correct price you should pay for your portion of the trip, I'll let you ride for free. Remember, your answer has to be mathematically equitable for all of us." How much should the students pay for their journey?

Of the four choices below, which best completes this figure analogy?

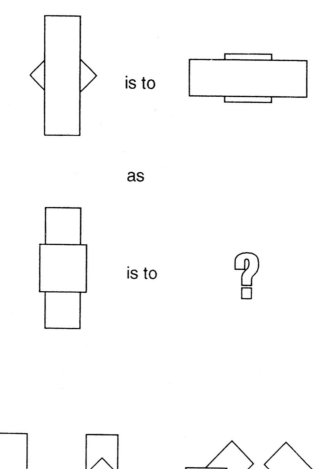

A   B   C   D

Of the four choices below, which best completes this figure analogy?

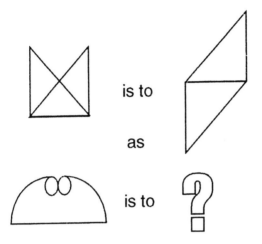

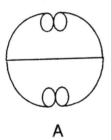 is to

as

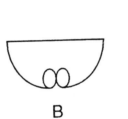 is to

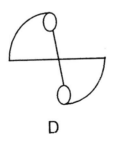

A   B   C

D

44

Which of the five choices completes this analogy?

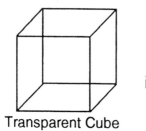

Transparent Cube

is to

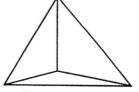

Transparent Tetrahedron

as

is to

A

B

C

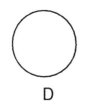

D

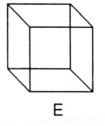

E

Complete this analogy.

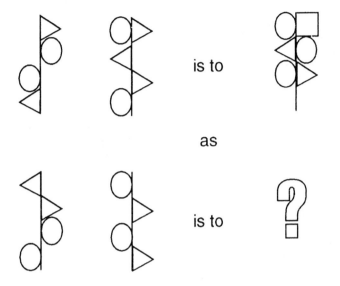

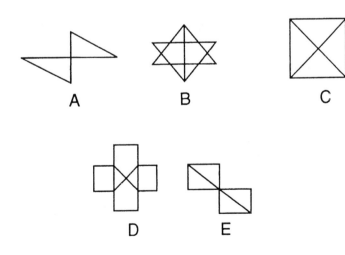

46

Which one of the following figures does not belong? Hint: Don't consider symmetry.

A　　　B　　　C

D　　　E

47

A northbound freight train with 100 boxcars will soon meet a southbound freight train with 100 boxcars in single-track territory. They'll meet near a siding track that has a maximum capacity of 80 boxcars. The engines of the southbound train are too heavy to enter any portion of the siding trackage.

With the following information, is it possible for the two trains to get around each other and continue on their trip in the same direction as they started? If so, how?

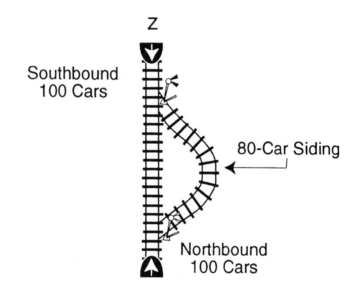

Basic RR Rules

No cars may roll freely by themselves.
All cars and engines have couplers on both ends.

The siding track has switches on both ends.
Engines can move in either direction.
Both trains have radio communications and cabooses.

Find the hidden phrase or title.

Find the hidden phrase or title.

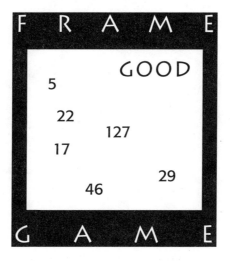

An old puzzle asks how many revolutions a rotating coin can make around a duplicate fixed coin in one full rotation. The answer is two. This is a variation of that puzzle, and you may be surprised at the answer.

A rotating gear in a diesel engine revolves around two fixed gears and looks like this.

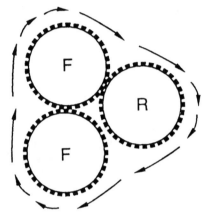

All three gears are identical in size. How many revolutions will Gear R make in one full rotation around the fixed gears?

 51

Sara rows down the Snake River at a rate of 4 m.p.h. with the current. After she's traveled for two hours, she turns around and rows back against the current to where she started. It takes her four hours to return. What is Sara's rowing rate in still water? What is the rate of the Snake River?

 52

Candace is Jane's daughter's aunt's husband's daughter's sister. What is the relationship between Candace and Jane?

53

English puzzler Henry Dudeney was a master at creating all types of intriguing train puzzles. From the speeds of roaring locomotives to the times on station clocks, his train puzzles demonstrated elegant simplicity while testing the solver's deductive reasoning power.

In keeping with the spirit of Dudeney's train puzzles, Professor Fractal was taking his best math-prize student to Kensington Station to board a train for Leeds, for the British Isles Math Contest. As they entered the depot, the station clock chimed six o'clock. The professor turned to his math whiz and said, "If you can tell me at what time, immediately prior to six o'clock, the hands of the clock were exactly opposite each other, I'll buy you dinner before your departure."

The student enjoyed a delicious London broil. What was the exact time in hours, minutes, and seconds when the hands of the clock were opposite each other, immediately prior to six o'clock?

 54

See if you can deduce the logic of the letters in and around the circles to determine what the missing letter is inside the last circle.

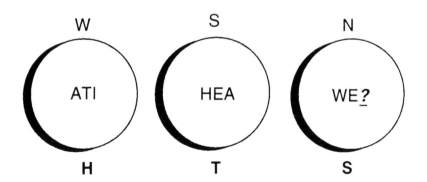

55

What's the missing number?

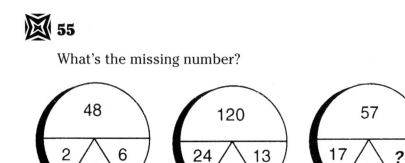

 56

If one type of weight can balance either 5 gold coins or 4 silver coins, then ten weights of the same type can balance 20 gold coins and how many silver coins in the same scale pan?

57

Sometimes in school or business, we are given information that looks impossible to decipher, only to find out that applying a little "elbow grease" aids in sorting things out. Below are several statements that attempt to form some relationships between the letters A, B, C, and D, and the numbers 1, 2, 3, and 4. Using the following information, see if you can straighten out this confusion and identify each letter with its associated number.

> If A is 1, then B is not 3.
> If B is not 1, then D is 4.
> If B is 1, then C is 4.
> If C is 3, then D is not 2.
> If C is not 2, then D is 2.
> If D is 3, then A is not 4.

Hint: Make a grid with A, B, C, and D on one side and 1, 2, 3, and 4 on the other. Then make some assumptions.

58

Linda wants to drain the water out of a 55-gallon barrel. She has the choice of using either a 2-inch-diameter hose or two 1-inch-diameter hoses to drain the barrel. Which will drain the barrel faster—the 2-inch hose or the two 1-inch hoses? Will they drain the water equally fast?

59

It seems that every puzzle writer has a friend who is a brilliant logician and who makes a living solving impossible problems for the government or tracking down criminals.

Molly O'Coley is of that rare breed. The 'Mazin' Ms. Molly, as she's known to Scotland Yard, sent me a note some time ago about a notorious international criminal who was jailed due to her efforts. Much secrecy had surrounded the trial because the prosecution didn't want the public to know the large sum of money recovered by Ms. Molly. They felt that information might hinder future efforts to bring the criminal's associates to trial.

Below is the total contents of Ms. Molly's note to me. Each letter of this note stands for a number, and the total is the sum that Ms. Molly recovered. Can you find the exact amount?

$$\begin{array}{r} \text{TRAIL} \\ + \text{TRIAL} \\ \hline \text{GUILTY} \end{array}$$

$$Y = 3$$

Note: The letter Y is not part of the addition problem. I later discovered that the Y = 3 also indicated the number of associates the criminal had. Ms. Molly found them in Stuttgart and had them extradited to London.

60

In this alphametic, if you find that one of the letters is equal to nine, then another letter must equal 5 and still another must be 4. Let E = 4 and V = 7.

$$
\begin{array}{cr}
A & FIVE \\
+ A & FOUR \\
\hline
IF & NINE
\end{array}
$$

 61

After trying several times to reach my wife by phone and failing, due to problems with the telephone, I arrived home to find this curious coded message left next to the telephone. Can you decipher my wife's message?

9368 86 289 2 639 74663

 62

There are 100 students applying for summer jobs in a university's geology/geography department. Ten of the students have never taken a course in geology or geography. Sixty-three of the students have taken at least one geology course. Eighty-one have taken at least one geography course.

What is the probability that of the 100 applicants any student selected at random has taken either geography or geology, but not both?

How many students have taken at least one course in both geology and geography?

63

Find the hidden phrase or title.

 64

Here's another old puzzle with a different twist. Two friends were talking, and the first one said, "Do you remember the brainteaser about a drawer full of black and blue socks?" His friend replied he wasn't sure. "The object is to determine the minimum number of socks you'd have to pick in the dark in order to have a pair of the same color," said the first friend. "Yes," said the second friend, "I remember. The answer is three." "That's right," replied the storyteller. "Quickly now, tell me the minimum number of socks you'd need to take from the drawer if it contained twenty-four blue socks and twenty black socks and you wanted to be assured of a pair of black socks?"

 65

$(17{:}8) : (25{:}7) :: (32{:}5) : (\underline{\quad ? \quad} : \underline{\quad ? \quad})$

66

Find the hidden phrase or title.

 67

At a gathering of mathematicians, everyone shook hands with four other people, except for two people, who shook hands with only one other person.

If one person shakes hands with another, each person counts as one handshake.

What is the minimum number of people who could have been present? What is the total number of handshakes that took place?

 68

You've just thrown your first two dice in a craps game and your point is 10. This means that you must continue to roll the dice until you roll another 10 to make your point. If you roll a 7 before you roll another 10, you lose.

What are your chances of winning with 10 as your point?

The numbers 1 through 6 are arranged so that any number resting between and below two other numbers is the difference between those two numbers.

Using numbers 1 through 10, fill in the X's below to create a "difference triangle" with the same conditions. If you'd like a little stiffer challenge, try this using the numbers 1 through 15 in five rows.

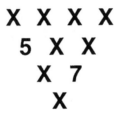

70

This puzzle is a variation of the game nim, named by Harvard mathematics professor Charles Bouton in 1901. Mathemagician Martin Gardner discusses a version of the game in his book *Entertaining Mathematical Puzzles*.

In Gardner's version, coins are arranged like this:

Two players take turns removing the coins. More than one coin can be removed on a turn as long as they are in the same row. The person who is forced to take the last coin is the loser. Gardner asks the reader if an ironclad winning first move can be determined. The answer is yes. The first player removes three coins from the bottom row.

In our version of nim, an extra coin is added to the top so that the ten coins are arranged like this.

The rules are basically the same, except that in our game, if more than one coin is removed from any row, the coins must be adjacent to each other. For example, if a coin had been removed from the bottom row by a player, the other player may *not* pick up the remaining three coins.

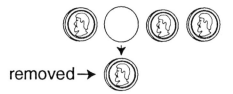

In this case, the second player may pick up the coin on the left or either or both on the right. In our version, there are two winning first moves. What are they?

Logician George Summers's puzzles are among the best. His logic brainteasers offer a clear, straightforward presentation of the puzzle, yet fully test the deductive reasoning process of even the best puzzle enthusiasts. His book *The Great Book of Mind Teasers & Mind Puzzlers* will keep you busy for days.

In one of his creations, which could be called the "letter cross," letters represent numbers, and you must make several deductions to come up with the value of each letter.

Here is a version of a letter cross puzzle. Although not particularly difficult, it still requires several steps for its solution. Solve this, and you'll be ready to tackle some of Summers's crunchers.

$$\textbf{A B C D}$$
$$\textbf{E}$$
$$\textbf{F}$$
$$\textbf{G H I J}$$

$$\textbf{A} + \textbf{B} + \textbf{C} + \textbf{D} = \textbf{D} + \textbf{E} + \textbf{F} + \textbf{G} = \textbf{G} + \textbf{H} + \textbf{I} + \textbf{J} = 17$$

A = 4 and J = 0. Using all digits from 0 through 9 only once, find the values for B, C, D, E, F, and G.

There is more than one correct answer. Several numbers are interchangeable.

Here's a punchy clue to a series question.

Cubes and squares can be one and the same,
But if this so happens, they need a new name.
Squbes sounds OK, so I'll leave it at that,
But can you now tell me where the next one is at?

$$\textbf{64} \quad \textbf{729} \quad \textbf{4,096} \quad \textbf{15,625} \quad \underline{\;\;\textbf{?}\;\;}$$

There are five boxes such that Box C fits into Box A, Box D fits into Box B or Box C, and Box A is not the largest.

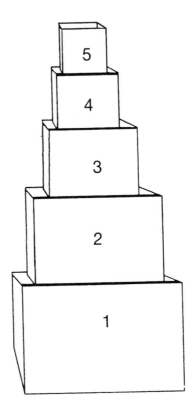

As you can see, Box 1 is the largest and each progressive box is smaller, so that Box 5 is the smallest. The number of the box that represents Box A plus the number of the box that represents Box E is equal to the number of the box that represents Box D plus the number of the box that represents Box C. Determine the size of Boxes A through E from largest to smallest.

Three identical bags contain colored balls. Each bag has one red and one white ball. A ball is drawn out of Bag 1, another out of Bag 2, and another out of Bag 3.

What are the chances that you'll end up with exactly 2 white balls?

| Bag 1 | Bag 2 | Bag 3 |

75

Three straight cuts on a single plane through a cube will result in a maximum of eight pieces. What is the maximum number of pieces that will result when four planar cuts are made through a cube? The slices may not be rearranged between cuts.

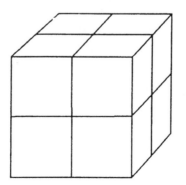

Take three coins and arrange them like this.

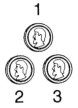

Now, if you wanted to turn the triangle upside down using the minimum number of moves, you would move Coin 1 below Coins 2 and 3 like this.

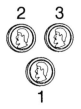

What is the minimum number of coins you need to move to turn the following triangle upside down?

Can you find a general pattern or formula for predicting how many coins you must move to turn any triangle of N length upside down?

This game, often called the triangle pegboard game, has been around a long time and offers a good challenge. Maybe you've seen it in restaurants throughout the country.

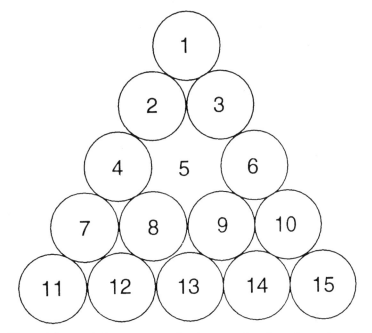

The object of the game, which can also be played with coins, is to jump one peg over another, staying inside the triangle. After jumping over a peg, remove that peg. The goal is to end up with only one peg. Begin with 14 pegs or coins and leave the middle hole open. There is only one solution (two if you count its mirror image). If you've tried this puzzle, you know that it can drive you crazy if you get off on the wrong track.

On the next page are the first six moves towards the correct solution. Of course, if you want to go it alone, stop reading here.

Take fourteen markers or coins and arrange them as shown. Don't forget to remove a marker after you've jumped over it.

Here's your start.

Step 1—Move 12 to 5.
Step 2—Move 10 to 8.
Step 3—Move 14 to 12.
Step 4—Move 3 to 10.
Step 5—Move 2 to 9.
Step 6—Move 7 to 2.

There are thirteen jumps in all. The remaining seven moves are in the Answers section.

 78

Imagine that you must build a tunnel through eight identical cubes. The tunnel must be continuous and start from any of the three exposed faces of Cube 1. The tunnel has to pass through each of the eight cubes only once, and it cannot cut through any place where more than two cubes meet. How many cubes must be excluded as the tunnel's final or exit cube? What are their numbers?

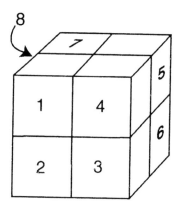

Below are five different sides of a solid object constructed out of several identical cubes fused together. What does the sixth side look like?

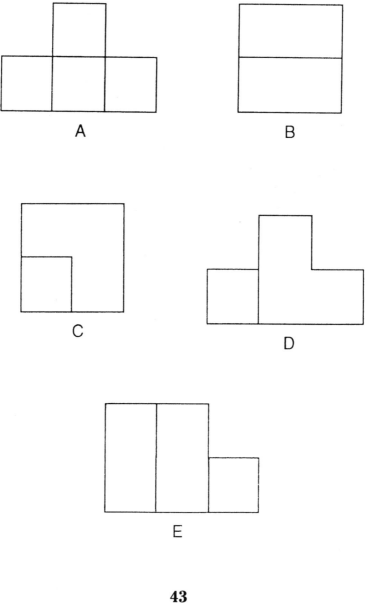

80

Find the hidden phrase or title.

 81

Arrange twelve toothpicks into a sort of window pane. Rearrange only three of them to create ten different triangles of any size.

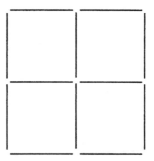

82

Find the hidden phrase or title.

 83

Four friends, Bob, Bill, Pat, and Tom, are nicknamed Rabbit, Walleye, Fly, and Bear—but not necessarily in that order.

a. Pat can run faster than Rabbit, but can't lift as much weight as Fly.

b. Rabbit is stronger than Tom, but slower than Walleye.

c. Bob is faster than both Pat and Bear, but not as strong as Rabbit.

What is the nickname of each friend?

 84

A certain blend of grass seed is made by mixing Brand A at $9.00 a pound with Brand B at $4.00 a pound. If the blend is worth $7.00 a pound, how many pounds of Brand A are needed to make 40 pounds of the blend?

85

Two rockets are launched simultaneously from two different positions.

Rocket A will land at the same spot from which Rocket B was launched, and Rocket B will land at the same spot where Rocket A was launched, allowing a small distance to the left or right to avoid a midair collision.

The rockets are launched from the same angle, and therefore travel the same distance both vertically and horizontally. If the rockets reach their destinations in one and nine hours, respectively, after passing each another, how much faster is one rocket than the other?

A   B

 86

Your chemistry teacher asks you to convert temperatures from one system of measurement to another. These are new systems for determining temperatures, so the classic conversions from Centigrade, Fahrenheit, and Kelvin don't apply.

You are told that 14° in the first system is equal to 36° in the second system. You also know that 133° in the first system is equal to 87° in the second.

What is the method or formula for converting one system to the other?

At what temperature will both thermometers read the same?

87

Here is a sequence of five figures. What would the sixth figure look like?

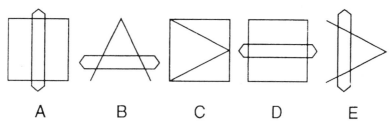

A   B   C   D   E

88

One of these figures doesn't belong with the rest. Don't be concerned about symmetry. Which doesn't belong? Why?

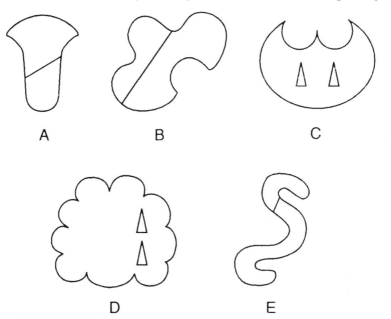

A   B   C

D   E

89

Apollona Constantino has 57 of them. Maggie Lieber has 36 of them. Paul Furstenburg has 45 of them. Based on the above, how many of them does Mary Les have?

How many individual cubes are in this configuration? All rows and columns in the figure are complete unless you actually see them end.

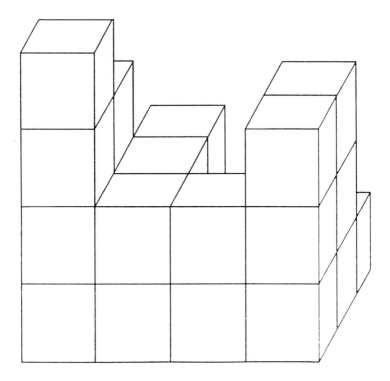

 91

Thirteen boys and girls wait to take their seats in the same row in a movie theater. The row is thirteen seats long. They decide that after the first person sits down, the next person has to sit next to the first. The third sits next to one of the first two and so on until all thirteen are seated. In other words, no person except the first can take a seat with empty seats on both sides.

How many different ways can this be accomplished, assuming that the first person can choose any of the thirteen seats?

92

Three dollar bills were exchanged for a certain number of nickels and the same number of dimes. How many nickels were there? Read this puzzle to a group of friends and see how long it takes to come up with the answer. You may be surprised!

 93

In the multiplication puzzle below, *x*, *y*, and *z* represent different digits. What is the sum of *x*, *y*, and *z*?

$$\begin{array}{r} yx \\ \times\ 7 \\ \hline zxx \end{array}$$

 94

Alex, Ryan, and Steven are sports fans. Each has a different favorite sport among football, baseball, and basketball. Alex does not like basketball; Steven does not like basketball or baseball. Name each person's favorite sport.

 95

Let's say 26 zips weigh as much as 4 crids and 2 wobs. Also, 8 zips and 2 crids have the same weight as 2 wobs. How many zips have the weight of 1 wob?

96

Find the hidden phrase or title.

F R A M E

Look U Leap

G A M E

 97

There is a certain logic shared by the following four circles. Can you determine the missing number in the last circle?

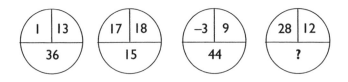

1	13
36	

17	18
15	

−3	9
44	

28	12
?	

 98

What is $\frac{1}{2}$ of $\frac{2}{3}$ of $\frac{3}{5}$ of 240 divided by $\frac{1}{2}$?

99

Find the hidden phrase or title.

 100

The three words below can be rearranged into two words that are also three words! Can you decipher this curious puzzle?

the red rows

 101

Can you determine the next letter in the following series?

A   C   F   H   K   M   ?

102

One of the figures below lacks a common characteristic that the other five figures have. Which one is it and why?

Hint: This does not have to do with right angles or symmetry.

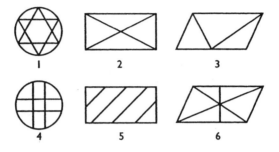

 **103**

Find the hidden phrase or title.

104

A car travels from point A to point B (a distance of one mile) at 30 miles per hour. How fast would the car have to travel from point B to point C (also a distance of one mile) to average 60 miles per hour for the entire trip?

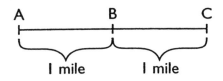

 105

Try your luck at this "trickle-down" puzzle. Starting at the top, change one letter of each succeeding word to arrive at the word at the bottom.

T O O K

_____

_____

_____

B U R N

 106

If the length of a rectangle is increased by 25 percent and its width is decreased by 25 percent, what is the percentage of change in its area?

107

A friend has a bag containing two cherry gumdrops and one orange gumdrop. She offers to give you all the gumdrops you want if you can tell her the chances of drawing a cherry gumdrop on the first draw and the orange gumdrop on the second draw. Can you meet your friend's challenge?

108

The design on the left is made up of three paper squares of different sizes, one on top of the other. What is the minimum number of squares needed to create the design on the right?

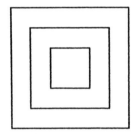 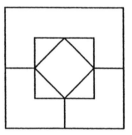

109

Here's a variation on an old classic. On what side of the line does the "R" go?

A B D   O P Q
C E F G H I J K L M N

110

Find the hidden phrase or title.

FRAME

TIME
FUTURE

GAME

 111

Given the initial letters of the missing words, complete this sentence.

There are 100 Y in a C.

 112

If I tripled one-quarter of a fraction and multiplied it by that fraction, I would get one-twelfth. What is the original fraction?

113

Two toy rockets are heading directly for each other. One is traveling at 50 miles per hour and the other is traveling at 70 miles per hour. How far apart will these two rockets be one minute before they collide?

 114

Find the hidden phrase or title.

 115.

Think of five squares that are the same size. In how many ways can these five squares be combined, edge to edge? (No mirror images allowed.)

 116

What number is four times one-third the number that is one-sixteenth less than three-thirty-seconds?

117

Below are five words. By adding the same three letters at the beginning of each word, you can come up with five new words. What three letters will do the trick?

HER

ION

OR

IF

TO

 118

If x^2 is larger than 9, which of the following is true?

a. x is greater than 0.

b. 0 is greater than x.

c. x is equal to 0.

d. x^3 is greater than 0.

e. There is insufficient information to determine a solution.

119

Based on the following information, how many pleezorns does Ahmad Adziz have?

Molly O'Brien has 22 pleezorns.

Debbie Reynolds has 28 pleezorns.

Roberto Montgomery has 34 pleezorns.

120

What is 10 percent of 90 percent of 80 percent?

 121

Find the hidden phrase or title.

 122

A mixture of chemicals costs $40 per ton. It is composed of one type of chemical that costs $48 per ton and another type of chemical that costs $36 per ton. In what ratio were these chemicals mixed?

123

Find the hidden phrase or title.

 124

How many triangles of any size are in the figure below?

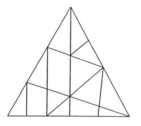

 125

If the ratio of $5x$ to $4y$ is 7 to 8, what is the ratio of $10x$ to $14y$?

126

Decipher the following cryptogram:

WLA'P XLJAP RLJO XGMXBSAE NSQLOS PGSR GCPXG.

 127

Find the hidden phrase or title.

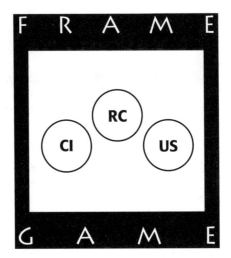

 128

How many four-letter words can you find in the word "twinkle"? (Try for at least 15.)

 129

Do this quickly: Write down twelve thousand twelve hundred twenty-two.

130

Below are four sets of letters that are related in a way known to virtually everyone. Can you find the missing two letters? (*Hint:* Some people have been known to take months to solve this!)

ON
DJ
FM
AM
? ?

 131

Find the hidden phrase or title.

132

Find the hidden phrase or title.

 133

In the strange land of Doubledown the alphabet appears to be hieroglyphics, but it isn't really much different from ours. Below is one of the Doubledown months spelled out. Which month of ours is comparable?

JOKE

134

Which is larger, $3^7 + 7^3$ or the sum of $4^6 + 6^4$? No calculators, please.

135

Unscramble this word:

GORNSIMMAROCI

 136

Given the initial letters of the missing words, complete this sentence.

There is one W on a U.

137

Below are six rays. Choosing two of the rays, how many angles of less than 90 degrees can you form? (Angle ACB is less than 90 degrees.)

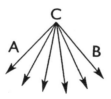

138

By arranging all nine integers in a certain order, it is possible to come up with fractions equal to $\frac{1}{2}$, $\frac{1}{3}$, $\frac{1}{4}$, $\frac{1}{5}$, $\frac{1}{6}$, $\frac{1}{7}$, $\frac{1}{8}$ and $\frac{1}{9}$. See if you can come up with one of these.

$$\text{Example: } \frac{1}{8} = \frac{3,187}{25,496}$$

139

Find the hidden phrase or title.

F R A M E

ieieieceieiei

G A M E

 140

What are the two missing numbers in the series below?

8, 15, 10, 13, 12, 11, 14, 9, 16, 7, ?, ?

 141

What is the value of *z* in the following problem? (Each number is a positive integer between 0 and 9.)

$$\begin{array}{r} x \\ y \\ +z \\ \hline xy \end{array}$$

142

Referring back to the last puzzle, where **z** was found to be 9, what is the value of **x**?

$$\begin{array}{r} x \\ y \\ +z \\ \hline xy \end{array}$$

 143

Most of us know the following rules of divisibility:

A number is divisible by 2 if it ends in an even digit.

A number is divisible by 3 if the sum of its digits is divisible by 3.

Is there such a rule for dividing by 8?

 144

Which one of the following five words doesn't belong with the others, and why?

Pail
Skillet
Knife
Suitcase
Doorbell

 145

If you wrote down all the numbers from 5 to 83, how many times would you write the number 4?

146

Four of the figures below share a characteristic that the fifth figure doesn't have. Can you determine which figure doesn't go with the others and why?

A   B   C   D   E

 147

Find the hidden phrase or title.

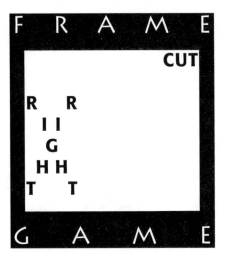

 148

A certain barrel of candy can be equally divided (without cutting pieces) between five, seven, or thirteen people. What is the least number of pieces of candy the barrel could contain?

149

Find the hidden phrase or title.

F R A M E

BLANK
fill
BLANK
fill
BLANK

G A M E

 150

Which is greater, 107 percent of 300 or 50 percent of 600?

 151

What is the value of the following?

$$\frac{1}{3 + \dfrac{1}{3^{1}/_{3}}}$$

152

The diagram below is the beginning of a "magic square" in which all rows and columns and both diagonals add up to 34. Can you fill in the rest of the numbers?

1	8	13	12
14			
4		16	
15			

 153

The diagram below can be drawn without lifting your pencil or crossing any other line. Can you do it?

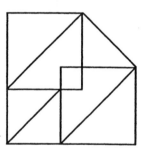

 154

Imagine that a coin called a "kookla" is equal in value to either 7 gold pieces or 13 silver pieces. If you have 40 kooklas that you want to exchange for both silver and gold pieces and your bank has only 161 gold pieces on hand, how many silver pieces should you expect to receive with the 161 gold pieces?

155

The two numbers in each box have the same relationship to each other as do the two numbers in every other box. What is the missing number?

| 3, 8 | −5, 24 | 0, −1 | 9, 80 | 6, ? |

 156

There are six chairs, each of a different color. In how many different ways can these six chairs be arranged in a straight line?

 157

Find the hidden phrase or title.

158

Do the numbers 9 and 10 go above or below the line?

1	2				6		
		3	4	5		7	8

 159

Find the hidden phrase or title.

 160

A concept that math students often find difficult to understand is that a negative multiplied by a negative results in a positive (example: –5 × –5 = 25). Can you come up with a real-life example, in words, to illustrate this?

161

Unscramble the following word:

RGAALEB

 162

Without using + or – signs, arrange five 8s so that they equal 9.

 163

How many individual cubes are in the configuration below? (All rows and columns run to completion unless you see them end.)

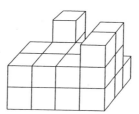

 164

How many different words can you make from the word "Thanksgiving"? You might be surprised to find how many new words can be made from a word that doesn't contain the letter "e."

 165

What is $^1/_{10}$ divided by $^1/_2$ divided by $^1/_5$ times $^7/_9$?

166

Find the hidden phrase or title.

 167

When the proper weights are assigned, this mobile is perfectly balanced. Can you determine the three missing weights?

(*Hint:* Try starting with the 8-foot section of the mobile. Remember that Distance × Weight = Distance × Weight.)

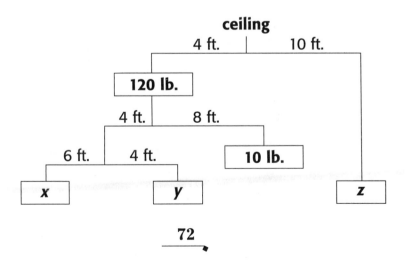

168

Below are two numbers represented by *x* and *y*.
Regardless of the values of *x* and *y*, all possible answers
resulting from the difference in these two numbers share
one unique characteristic. What is it?

$$xy$$
$$-yx$$
$$??$$

 169

The perimeter of a square has a value that is two-thirds of
the number representing its square footage. What is the
size of the square?

 170

Find the hidden phrase or title.

171

In the game of craps, what are the chances that you will be a winner on your first roll by getting either a 7 or an 11?

 172

Find the hidden phrase or title.

Calm   Storm

 173

Here's another four-letter "trickle-down" puzzle. Find the three missing words, each with only one letter changed from the previous word, to arrive at **BARN**.

M O O D
_____
_____
_____
B A R N

174

What is the value of T in the following puzzle?

$$A + B = H$$
$$H + P = T$$
$$T + A = F$$
$$B + P + F = 30$$
$$A = 2$$

 175

If five potatoes and six onions cost $1.22 and six potatoes and five onions cost $1.31, what does an onion cost?

 176

Find the hidden phrase or title.

Below are 10 matchsticks of equal length. By moving 2 and only 2 matchsticks, can you create 2 squares only, with no leftover matchsticks?

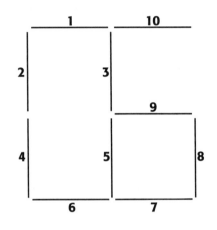

 178

A bag contains 7 green balls and 3 red ones. What is the probability of randomly taking out 3 green balls in succession without looking if:

A: Each ball is replaced before the next draw?

B: The balls are not replaced?

179

Find the missing number in the following series:

$$^{20}/_{48} \quad ^{1}/_{3} \quad ^{1}/_{4} \quad ^{1}/_{6} \quad ^{1}/_{12} \quad ?$$

180

Find the hidden phrase or title.

 181

Given the initial letters of the missing words, complete this sentence.

There are 206 B in the H B.

 182

What is the first number having factors that add up to more than the number itself? (Don't include the number itself as one of the factors.)

 183

What number is ¼ of ⅓ of ⅙ of 432, divided by ⅓?

184

Find the hidden phrase or title.

 185

One hundred people are applying for a sales position that would require them to sell both golf equipment and athletic shoes. Thirteen of the applicants have no prior experience in sales. Sixty-five of the applicants have previously sold golf equipment, and 78 of the applicants have sold athletic shoes. How many of the applicants have experience in selling both golf equipment and athletic shoes?

 186

What's the difference between 11 yards square and 11 square yards?

187

Find the four-letter word that will make new words when added in front of these:

**GUARD
LONG
TIME**

 188

Find the hidden phrase or title.

 189

What is the first year after the year 2000 in which the numbers of the year will read the same right-side-up and upside-down? What is the second year in which this will occur? (No fair using digital numerals, like 2!)

190

H is to one as C is to six as N is to ?

 191

Find the hidden phrase or title.

 192

A "perfect" number is a number whose factors add up to the number (not including the number itself). For example:

The factors of 6 are 3, 2, and 1 and 3 + 2 + 1 = 6.

The factors of 28 are 14, 7, 4, 2, and 1 and 14 + 7 + 4 + 2 + 1 = 28.

What are the next two perfect numbers?

 193

What are the chances of flipping a penny four times and getting at least two tails?

194

Find the hidden phrase or title.

 195

Decipher the following cryptogram. Each letter represents another letter in the alphabet.

OTD X GACOT ST BPWF WASFTOOX.

 196

What is the next number in the following series?

1, 2, 6, 30, 60, 180, 900, 1,800, 5,400, —

197

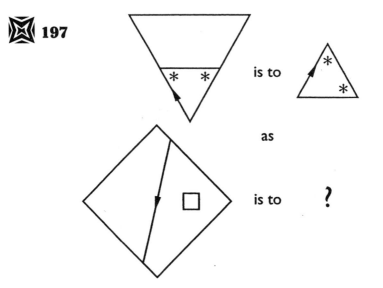

is to

as

is to **?**

 198

A pipe can fill a swimming pool in three hours. A second pipe can fill the pool in two hours. If both pipes are turned on at the same time, how long will it take them to fill the pool?

 199

I am ten years older than my sister. There was a time when I was three times older than she was, and in one year I will be twice as old as she is. What is my age now?

200

Here's an interesting twist on an old series puzzle. See if you can come up with the missing letter. (*Hint:* This problem is best approached with an even hand.)

T   F   S   E   T   T   F   ?

Find the hidden phrase or title.

 202

Susie's and Sally's last names are Billingsley and Jenkins, but not necessarily in that order. Two of the following statements are false. What is the real name of each person?

Susie's last name is Billingsley.
Susie's last name is Jenkins.
Sally's last name is Jenkins.

 203

Can you come up with a quick way to find the square of 95 mentally . . . or for that matter the square of 45, 55, 65, etc.?

Hint. Think of square numbers above and below each of these numbers.

There is more than one way to do this.

204.

If you find the correct starting point in the wheel below and move either clockwise or counterclockwise, the letters will spell out a common everyday word. What is the missing letter, and what is the word?

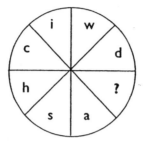

 205

Find the hidden phrase or title.

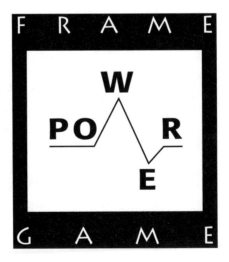

206

How many digits must be changed in the following addition problem to make the sum equal 245?

$$\begin{array}{r} 89 \\ 16 \\ +98 \\ \hline \end{array}$$

 207

In a certain box of candy, the number of caramels is 25 percent of the number of other candies in the box. What percentage of the entire box are the caramels?

 208

Find the hidden phrase or title.

209

Given the initial letters of the missing words, complete the following sentence. (Hint: Think of hydrogen.)

There are 106 E in the P T.

 210

Change one and only one letter in each successive word to come up with the next word:

R O A D
_____
_____
_____
L O O P

211

One of the following diagrams doesn't fit with the others. Which one is it? Why? Hint: Think symmetry.

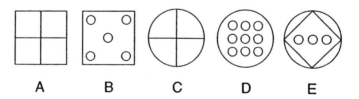

A   B   C   D   E

Here's fun with roman numerals. See if you can match column A to column B.

$\overline{V}$	100
$\overline{M}$	500
$\overline{C}$	1,000
C	5,000
$\overline{L}$	10,000
$\overline{X}$	50,000
$\overline{D}$	100,000
D	500,000
M	1,000,000

 213

Find the hidden phrase or title.

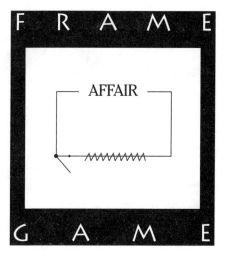

214

Using only the letters of the top row on a typewriter, how many 10-letter words can you create?

Remember, the letters are

Q W E R T Y U I O P

 215

Find the hidden phrase or title.

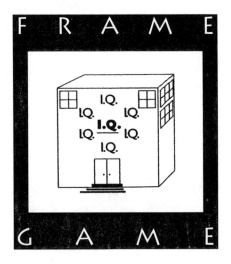

 216

In a certain game, a ball can fall through any of 50 holes evenly spaced around a wheel. The chance that a ball would fall into any one particular hole is 1 in 50. What are the chances that 2 balls circling the wheel at the same time would fall into the same hole?

217

What is the missing number in the following series?

$$84 \quad 12 \quad 2 \quad {}^{2}/_{5} \quad {}^{1}/_{10} \quad ?$$

 218

Find the hidden phrase or title.

 219

A man spent three-fourths of his money and then lost three-fourths of the remainder. He has $6 left. How much money did he start with?

 220

Molly and Maggie are Martha's mother's son's wife's daughters. What relation is Martha to Molly and Maggie?

221

In a foreign language, "rota mena lapy" means large apple tree, "rota firg" means small apple, and "mena mola" means large pineapple. Which word means tree?

 222

Unscramble the following word:

OMAHGOLR

 223

See if you can determine a relationship among the following circles to find the missing number in the last circle.

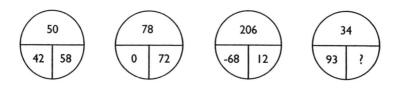

 224

What is the missing number in the following series?

(*Hint:* Could the numbers represent something other than quantities?)

13 9 14 4 — 2 5 14 4 9 14 ?

225

Find the hidden phrase or title.

 226

What familiar four-letter word can be placed in front of each of the following to form four new words?

Shelf
Worm
Mobile
Mark

 227

Given the initial letters of the missing words, complete this sentence:

There are 180 D in a T.

228

In a shuffled deck of 52 playing cards, you alone are picking the cards out of the deck, and the cards are face down. What are the odds of your drawing the Ace, King, Queen, and Jack of spades in succession:

1 chance in 208?
1 chance in 2,704?
1 chance in 6,497,400?
1 chance in 1,000,000,000?

 229

What number is 4 times $^1/_{10}$ the number that is $^1/_{10}$ less than $^3/_{13}$?

 230

There's an old puzzle that you have probably seen many times where you are asked to assign the same digit for each letter in the following.

$$\begin{array}{r} \text{SEND} \\ +\,\text{MORE} \\ \hline \text{MONEY} \end{array}$$

Now try this variation. Let M = 6 and N = 3.

$$\begin{array}{r} \text{SPEND} \\ -\,\text{MORE} \\ \hline \text{MONEY} \end{array}$$

231

How many different squares (of any size) are in this figure?

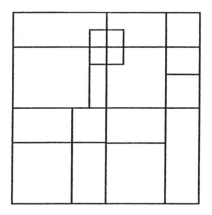

 232

Find the hidden phrase or title.

233

Decipher the following cryptogram:

SALTS LA ELLG

 234

Use three moves to get from the first word to the last.

B I K E

_____

_____

_____

M A T H

 235

The blank at the bottom of the second column below could be filled in by any one of three words. What are these words?

EVIL   **POST**
LIVE   **STOP**
VILE   **TOPS**
VEIL   _____

236

Here's a series problem that may require a little extra patience…

3 11 20 27 29 23 ?

 237

Unscramble this word:

A T T R E S P N A R N

 238

Find the hidden phrase or title.

240

A squash tournament has six rounds of single elimination for its singles competition. This includes the championship match, and there are no byes. How many players are entered when play begins?

 239

Given the initial letters of the missing words, complete the following sentence. (*Hint:* Think of Zorba.)

There are 24 L in the G A.

 241

What is the smallest number of square sheets of paper of any size that can be placed over each other to form the pattern below?

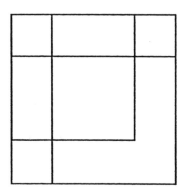

 242

If you built a four-sided pyramid—not counting the bottom as a side—using ping-pong balls, how many balls would be in a pyramid that had seven layers?

Find the hidden phrase or title.

 244.

Shown below is the bottom of a pyramid of black circles and white circles. The colors of the circles in each successive row are determined by the colors of the circles in the row below it. Complete the top three rows.

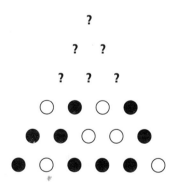

245

When the proper weights are assigned, the mobile shown here is in perfect balance. What are the four missing weights?

Hint: distance × weight = distance × weight.

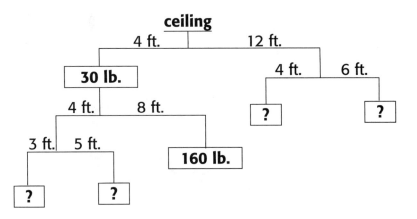

 246

Find the hidden phrase or title.

247

Four friends are going to a concert. When they arrive, there are only five seats together left in the theater. The manager will let all four friends in for free if one of them can tell her how many different seating arrangements are possible for four people with five empty seats. All four are let in free. Could you have given the correct answer?

 248

What word can be added to the end of each of the following words to form new words?

MOON
SHOE
MONKEY

 249

In a class of fewer than 30 students, two received a B on a math test, $1/7$ of the class received a C, $1/2$ received a D, and $1/4$ of the class failed the exam. How many students received an A?

 250

Molly can build a fence in two days. Alex can build the same fence in three days. Their younger brother, Steve, can build the fence in six days. If all three worked together, how long would it take to build the fence?

251

Find the hidden phrase or title.

F R A M E

corres4pondent

G A M E

 252

How many cubes of any size are in the configuration below? (*Hint:* Think of smaller, easier examples. There is an easily recognizable pattern to this puzzle.)

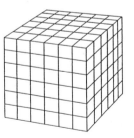

253

Arrange the numbers in the boxes so that no two consecutive numbers are next to each other (horizontally, vertically, or diagonally).

1	2	
3	4	5
6	7	8
	9	10

 254

If *p* is three-quarters of *q*, *q* is two-thirds of *r*, and *r* is one-half of *s*, what is the ratio of *s* to *p*?

 255

Find the hidden phrase or title.

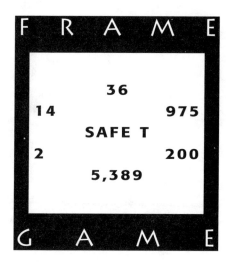

256

Four baseball players from the same team—Reggie, Chris, Lou, and Leo—play right field, first base, left field, and catcher, but none of the players and positions correspond in this order. From the following additional information, determine each player's position:

a) Reggie hits more homers than the catcher but fewer than the left fielder.

b) Leo and the left fielder are cousins.

 257

Find the hidden phrase or title.

 258

An eagle, an elephant, and a walleye have two each. A tiger, a moose, a bear, a turtle, and a snake have one each. Neither a human nor a gorilla has any. What are we talking about?

259

Here is a "trickle-down" puzzle. Simply replace one letter per line to arrive at the answer. If you can do it in fewer than the number of moves shown here, so much the better!

B A N D

———————

———————

———————

P I P S

 260

A bicycle is three times as old as its tires were when the bicycle was as old as the tires are now. What is the ratio of the tires' current age to the bicycle's current age?

 261

Quick now, which is bigger, 2^{13} or $2^{12} + 2^2$?

 262

Given the initial letters of the missing words, complete this phrase:

4 S and 7 Y A

263

Find the hidden phrase or title.

 264

Here's an alphametic for you:

Each letter represents a digit and the value for that letter remains the same throughout. No beginning letter of a word can be zero. Good luck!

$$
\begin{array}{r}
THREE \\
THREE \\
THREE \\
+\ ELEVEN \\
\hline
TWENTY
\end{array}
$$

The analogy puzzle below has a different twist. It is a spatial/visual analogy, and the answer is given! How are the Xs in the second grid of each analogy determined?

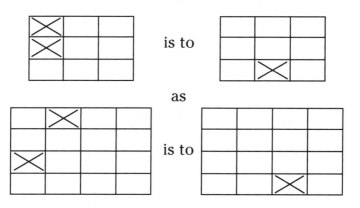

 266

Find the hidden phrase or title.

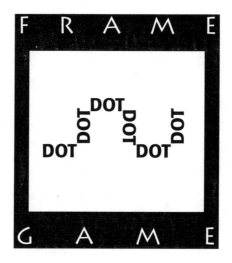

267

The starting lineup of a baseball team wants a photograph taken with all nine of the players sitting in a row on a bench. One of the ball players wonders how many different arrangements can be made of the order in which they sit. Do you know?

268

Below, on the left, is a list of words, some of which may be unfamiliar. On the right is a list of related, familiar words. Match the words in the second list to those in the first. Take each word on the left and look for the related words you know for sure. Then think of words that are similar to the ones you don't know—for instance, "potent" is like "potentate"—and then look for a reasonable match!

1. gambol	a. turtle
2. fortissimo	b. hats
3. sortie	c. loud
4. millinery	d. power
5. culinary	e. ambiguous
6. ornithology	f. smell
7. odoriferous	g. refined
8. gustatory	h. opposites
9. humus	i. cooking
10. terrapin	j. cow
11. bovine	k. frolic
12. antipodes	l. raid
13. equivocal	m. soil
14. potentate	n. birds
15. urbane	o. taste

269

A ladder was standing perfectly upright against a wall. Suddenly the foot of the ladder slid away from the wall and came to a stop 15 feet from the wall. The top of the ladder had moved only one-fifth of the ladder's length before it came to rest firmly on a windowsill. Do you have enough information to calculate the length of the ladder? If so, what is it?

 270

There are 10 krits in a flig, 6 fligs in a crat, 5 crats in a wirp, and 7 wirps in a nood. What is the number of krits in a nood divided by the number of fligs in a wirp?

 271

Find the hidden phrase or title.

272

Find the hidden phrase or title.

 273

What is 2,444 in Roman Numerals?

 274

Find the next two numbers in this series.

2 81 6 27 18 9 54 3 ? ?

275

Using any numeral four times and any mathematical symbols you choose, can you produce an equation that will yield the number 300?

 276

Suppose all counting numbers were arranged in columns as shown below. Under what letter would the number 100 appear?

A	B	C	D	E	F	G
1	2	3	4	5	6	7
8	9	10	11	12	13	14
15	16	17	—	—	—	—

 277

Nancy and Audrey set out to cover a certain distance by foot. Nancy walks half the distance and runs half the distance, but Audrey walks half the time and runs half the time. Nancy and Audrey walk and run at the same rate. Who will reach the destination first (or will it be a tie)?

 278

The following seven numbers share a unique property. What is it?

1961 6889 6119 8008 8118 6699 6009

279

Find the hidden phrase or title.

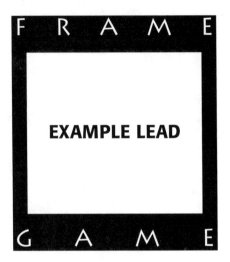

F R A M E

EXAMPLE LEAD

G A M E

 280

In the puzzle below, the numbers in the second row are determined by the relationships of the numbers in the first row. Likewise, the numbers in the third row are determined by the relationships of the numbers in the second row. Can you determine the relationships and find the missing number?

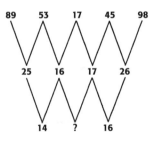

281

A mathematician's will stated that his wife should get one-third of his estate, his son one-fifth, his older daughter one-sixth, and his younger daughter $9,000. Who received more, his older daughter or his younger daughter?

 282

What single-digit number should go in the box with the question mark?

6	5	9	2	7
1	4	3	5	?
8	0	2	8	1

 283

There are 4 clocks in a room. One gains a minute every hour. Another loses a minute every hour. One runs backward at normal speed. The fourth always keeps the correct time. At 7:03 today, they all showed the same time, which was correct. When will this happen again?

284

Find the hidden phrase or title.

 285

While reading a newspaper you notice that four pages of one section are missing. One of the missing pages is page 5. The back page of this section is page 24. What are the other three missing pages?

 286

Suppose a, b, and c represent three positive whole numbers. If $a + b = 13$, $b + c = 22$, and $a + c = 19$, what is the value of c?

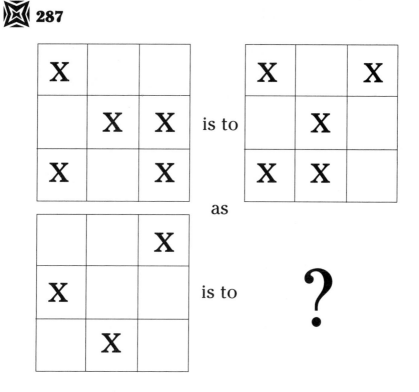

Below is a "trickle-down" word game. Change one letter and one letter only on each line to arrive at the word on the last line:

M O V E

_____

_____

_____

B A R K

289

Sarah is older than Julie and Maggie. Maggie is older than Paula. Ann is younger than Julie, but older than Paula. Ann is younger than Maggie. Sarah is younger than Liz. Who is the second oldest woman in this group?

 290

What is the missing number in the following series?

13 7 18 10 5 ? 9 1 12 6

 291

Find the hidden phrase or title.

292

How many triangles of any size are in the figure below?

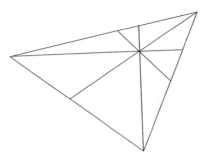

 293

Using four 4s and only four 4s, can you write an expression that equals 25? (There may be more than one way to accomplish this.)

 294

Find the hidden phrase or title.

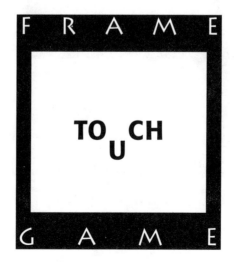

295

Which of the following is the smallest?

a. $\dfrac{\sqrt{10}}{10}$ b. $\dfrac{1}{10}$ c. $\sqrt{10}$

d. $\dfrac{1}{\sqrt{10}}$ e. $\dfrac{1}{10\sqrt{10}}$

 296

Find the hidden phrase or title.

 297

There are four colored pencils—two blue, one green, and one yellow. If you took two pencils from a drawer and you knew that one was blue, what would be the likelihood that the other pencil was also blue?

298

Unscramble this word: **KISDTYCRA**

 299

A certain blend of grass seed is made by mixing brand A ($8 a pound) with brand B ($5 a pound). If the blend is worth $6 a pound, how many pounds of brand A are needed to make 50 pounds of the blend?

 300

Find the hidden phrase or title.

 301

If you wrote down all the numbers from 1 to 100, how many times would you write the number 3?

302

Each of the following three words can have another three-letter word added to its beginning to form new words. Can you find at least one three-letter word to make this happen?

EAR
LESS
ANGER

 303

What is $^3/_4$ of $^1/_2$ of 4^2 minus $^1/_2$ of that result?

 304

Below are six discs stacked on a peg. The object is to reassemble the discs, one by one, in the same order on another peg, using the smallest number of moves. No larger disc can be placed on a smaller disc. How many moves will it take?

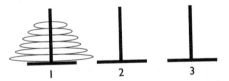

 305

From the word "service," see if you can create 15 new words.

306

Below is a list of numbers with accompanying codes. Can you decipher the code and determine the number on the last line?

Number	Code Number
589	521
724	386
1346	9764
?	485

 307

Which is greater, a single discount of 12 percent or two successive discounts of 6 percent—or are they the same?

 308

Find the hidden phrase or title.

309

Here's a fun and challenging puzzle for those who remember their algebra. Evaluate the following:

$$\frac{x+y}{x^2+y^2} \times \frac{x}{x-y} \div \frac{(x+y)^2}{x^4-y^4} - x$$

 310

Below is a sentence based on moving the letters of the alphabet in a consistent manner. See if you can crack the code and come up with the right answer.

BRX DUH D JHQLXV.

 311

The geometric figure below can be divided with one straight line into two parts that will fit together to make a perfect square. Draw that line by connecting two of the numbers.

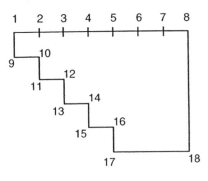

 312

What number logically comes next in the following sequence?

4 6 9 5 4 2 3 9 ?

313

Find the hidden phrase or title.

 314

Some pibs are dals.
All dals are zons.
Some zons are rews.
Some rews are dals.
Therefore, some pibs are definitely rews.

Is the above conclusion true or false?

 315

Which is larger: one-third times one-third of a dozen
dozen, or one-third dozen halved and cubed?

316

The *Genesee Flyer* leaves the station at 60 miles per hour. After three hours, the *Seneca Streamer* leaves the same station at 75 miles per hour, moving in the same direction on an adjacent track. Both trains depart the station at milepost 0. At what milepost will the *Streamer* draw even with the *Flyer*?

 317

A cyclist can ride four different routes from East Klopper to Wickly. There are eight different routes from Wickly to Ganzoon. From Ganzoon to Poscatool, there are three different routes. How many different combinations of routes from East Klopper to Poscatool can the cyclist take? (Do not consider going directly from East Klopper to Poscatool: all routes pass through Wickly, Ganzoon, and Poscatool.)

 318

The ratio of ³/₇ to ⁴/₉ is which of the following:

a. $\dfrac{8}{9}$

b. $\dfrac{35}{36}$

c. $\dfrac{3}{4}$

d. $\dfrac{27}{28}$

e. 1 to 1

319

Find the hidden phrase or title.

 320

Kelsey has flipped a penny 17 times in a row, and every time it has landed on heads. What are the chances that the next throw will land on heads?

 321

Can you place a symbol between the two numbers below to create a number greater than 4, but less than 5?

4 5

Below is a teeter-totter with a 5-pound weight placed 10 feet from the fulcrum and a 6-pound weight placed 5 feet from the fulcrum. On the right side of the fulcrum is a 16-pound weight that needs to be placed in order to balance the weights on the left side. How many feet from the fulcrum should the 16-pound weight be placed?

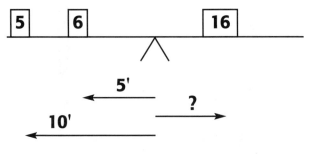

323

The following puzzle is one of analytical reasoning. See if you can determine the relationships between the figures and the words to find solutions to the two unknowns.

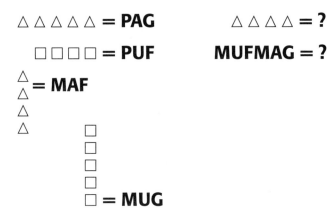

324

Find the hidden phrase or title.

F R A M E

projector
head

G A M E

 325

Given the initial letters of the missing words, complete this sentence.

It is 212 D F at which W B.

 326

Find the missing letter in the following series:

2 T 4 F 8 E 16 S 32 T 64 ?

327

See if you can match each word in the left-column with its meaning in the right-hand column:

1. **Unctuous**	a. **Study of the universe**
2. **Riparian**	b. **Relating to the bank of a lake or river**
3. **Porcine**	c. **An interlacing network, as of blood vessels**
4. **Plexus**	d. **An upright post**
5. **Platitude**	e. **Fertilize**
6. **Cosmology**	f. **Briskness**
7. **Concatenation**	g. **Relating to swine**
8. **Alacrity**	h. **A series connected by links**
9. **Fecundate**	i. **A trite remark**
10. **Newel**	j. **Oily**

 328

A box of chocolates can be divided equally among 3, 6, or 11 people. What is the smallest number of chocolates the box can contain?

329

Which figure does not belong with the other four figures?

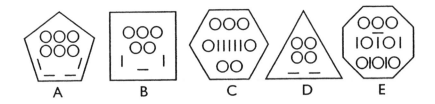

330

I recently returned from a trip. Today is Friday. I returned four days before the day after the day before tomorrow. On what day did I return?

 331

Find the hidden phrase or title.

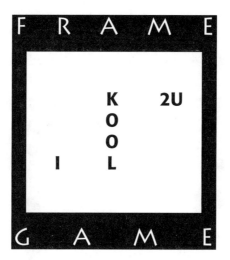

 332

A microscopic slide has 7,500 bacteria dying at a rate of 150 per hour. Another slide has 4,500 bacteria increasing at a rate of 50 per hour. In how many hours will the bacterial count on both slides be the same?

 333

A man told his friend, "Four years from now I'll be twice as old as I was fourteen years ago." How old is the man?

334

Which figure does not belong with the others, and why?

 335

Find the hidden phrase or title.

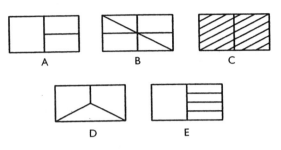

 336

The probability of drawing the Ace of Spades from a deck of 52 playing cards is 1 in 52. What is the probability of drawing the Ace, King, and Queen of Spades on three consecutive draws?

337

Sometimes things that are mathematically or scientifically true seem impossible. You may think this is one of them. Can you guess approximately how much a cubic yard of water weights?

17 pounds
170 pounds
1,700 pounds
500 pounds
98.8 pounds

 338

If a team wins 60 percent of its games in the first third of a season, what percentage of the remaining games must it win to finish the season having won 80 percent of the games?

 339

Given the initial letters of the missing words, complete the following sentence.

There are 50 S on the U S F.

 340

If ½ of 24 were 8, what would ⅓ of 18 be?

341

In this "trickle down" puzzle, you must change one letter of each succeeding word, starting at the top, to arrive at the word at the bottom. There may be more than one way to solve this—use your creativity!

P A R T

_____

_____

_____

W I N E

 342

Find the hidden phrase or title.

343

Solve this puzzle without using a pencil or calculator:

$$1 \times 1 = 1$$
$$11 \times 11 = 121$$
$$111 \times 111 = 12{,}321$$
$$1{,}111 \times 1{,}111 = ?$$

 344

Find the hidden phrase or title.

 345

There are six murks in a bop, eight bops in a farg, and three fargs in a yump. What is the number of murks in a yump divided by the number of bops in a yump?

346

What is the missing number in the triangle on the right?

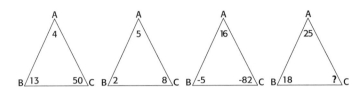

 347

If the volume of a cube is 729 cubic feet, how many cubic yards is it?

 348

If three pears and four oranges cost $.39 and four pears and three oranges cost $.38, how much does one pear cost?

 349

What is the missing number in this grid?

15	81	168
23	111	?
5	27	56

 350

If I quadrupled one-fifth of a fraction and multiplied it by that fraction, I would get one-fifth. What is the original fraction? (*Hint:* There are two answers.)

351

A six-piece band has agreed that the entire band will be paid $1,225 per gig. But the leader of the band is paid twice as much as each of the other five musicians. How much does the leader earn each gig?

 352

Find the hidden phrase or title.

 353

What's the missing number next to the letter "E"?

P7   H4   O6   N6   E?

354

Find the hidden phrase or title.

 355

In a foreign language, *fol birta klar* means "shine red apples." *Pirt klar farn* means "big red bicycles," and *obirts fol pirt* means "shine bicycles often." How would you say "big apples" in this language?

 356

Find three consecutive numbers such that the sum of the first number and the third number is 124.

 357

If 16_a = 20 and 36_a = 32, what does 26_a equal?

Find the hidden phrase or title.

359

What nine-letter word is written in the square below? You may start at any letter and go in any direction, but don't go back over any letter.

T   E   M

R   C   O

I   G   E

360

Can you position four squares of equal size in such a way that you end up with five squares of equal size?

361

At a reception, one-fourth of the guests departed at a certain time. Later, two-fifths of the remaining guests departed. Even later, three-fourths of those guests departed. If nine people were left, how many were originally at the party?

 362

Find the hidden phrase or title.

 363

In spelling out numbers, you don't often find the letter "a." Quickly now, what is the first number, counting upward from zero, in which this letter appears?

364

Find the hidden phrase or title.

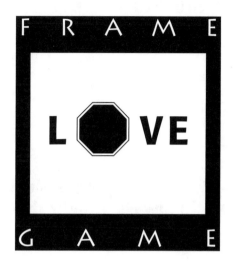

 365

With five fair tosses of a penny, what is the probability of its landing on heads five times in a row?

(*Hint:* Remember, the tosses constitute a sequence of events.)

 366

What physical characteristics do the following capital letters share in common?

A H I M O T U V W X Y

367

What comes next in the following series?

240 120 40 10 2 ?

 368

A triangle has sides of *X*, *Y*, and *Z*. Which of the following statements is true?

1. *X* – *Y* is always equal to 2.
2. *Y* – *X* is always less than *Z*.
3. *Z* – *X* is always greater than *Y*.
4. *X* + *Y* is always greater than *Z* + *Y*.
5. No correct answer is given.

 **369**

Find the hidden phrase or title.

370

Given four points in space and connecting three points at a time to determine a plane (extending to infinity), what is the maximum number of lines that will result from all intersections of the planes?

 371

What is the missing number in the circle below?

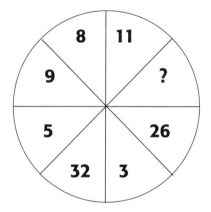

 372

When purchased together, a pair of binoculars and the case cost $100. If the binoculars cost $90 more than the case, how much does the case cost? Give yourself about 15 seconds to solve this.

 373

A cube measuring four inches on each side is painted blue all over and is then sliced into one-inch cubes. How many of the smaller cubes are blue on three sides?

374

In this "trickle-down" puzzle, start at the top and change one letter to each succeeding word to arrive at the word at the bottom.

F A S T

_____

_____

_____

M I N D

 375

A clock strikes six in five seconds. How long will it take to strike eleven?

 376

Find the hidden phrase or title.

377

Sammy Johnson has two sisters, but the Johnson girls have no brother. How can this be?

 378

Decipher this cryptogram:

T'M QPFASQ RS TD LATOPMSOLATP.
—G. N. KTSOMY

 379

Given the initial letters of the missing words, complete this sentence.

There are 9 I in a B G.

 380

What three-letter word can be placed in front of each of the following words to make four new words?

MAN
HOUSE
CAP
AM

381

Find the hidden phrase or title.

 382

Imagine we were to adopt a new number system based on 13 instead of 10. Show a way in which the first 13 numbers might be written.

 383

How many squares of any size are in the figure below? Be careful; there may be more than you think!

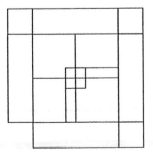

384

Electric current is measured in amps, resistance is measured in ohms, and power is measured in watts. What is frequency measured in?

 385

Find the hidden phrase or title.

 386

Unscramble the following word:

LAMPANETRYARI

 387

How would you write 944 in Roman numerals?

388

What is the missing letter in the last circle?

 389

If 2,048 people entered a statewide singles tennis tournament, how many total matches would be played, including the championship match?

 390

Decipher this cryptogram phrase:

SEO LXABXGS JW EMLLGQOBB.

 391

What four-letter word can be placed in front of each of the following words to form new words?

LINE
PHONE
WATERS

392

Find the hidden phrase or title.

 393

The numbers in each box below have a relationship in common. Can you identify that relationship and find the missing number?

2, 11	4, 67	5, 128	3, ?

 394

If you have a two-in-five chance of winning something, what are your odds?

395

How many triangles can you find in this diagram?

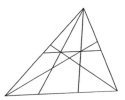

 396

Find the hidden phrase or title.

 397

Complete the following analogy:

B-sharp is to C as Bach is to ?

398

See if you can match the legal terms in the left column with the definitions in the right column:

1. Arbitration

2. Exculpatory

3. Judicial notice

4. Laches

5. Probative

6. Tort

7. Mediation

a. A rule in which the court takes notice of facts that are known with certainty to be true

b. Submission of controversies to a third party, whose decisions are usually binding

c. A doctrine providing a party an equitable defense where neglected rights are sought to be enforced against the party

d. A method of settling disputes with a neutral party in which the neutral party is a link between the disputing parties

e. A type of evidence that tends to clear or excuse a defendant from fault

f. Tending to prove a proposition or to persuade one of the truth of an allegation

g. A private or civil wrong

 399

The series below, containing the numbers 1 through 10, can be completed by placing the missing numbers, 2 and 3, at the end. Which comes first, the 2 or the 3? Why?

8   5   4   9   1   7   6   10   ?   ?

 400

How many different words can you make from the word "numbers"?

401

Find the hidden phrase or title.

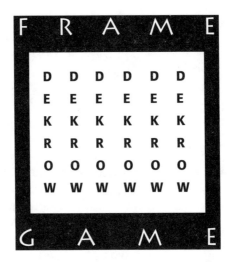

 402

Which figure below does not belong with the rest, and why?

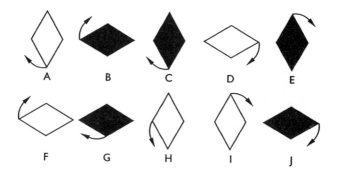

403

Given the initial letters of the missing words, complete this sentence.

There are 6 P on the S of D.

 404

Find the hidden phrase or title.

 405

What is the value of Z in the diagram below?

12   18   26   38   49
  X   8   X   X
    X   X   X
      X   X
        Z

406

Here's a four-letter "trickle-down" puzzle. See if you can come up with the three missing words, each with only one letter changed from the previous word, to arrive at the word PREP. (There may be more than one set of correct answers.)

F E A R

———————

———————

———————

P R E P

 407

Find the hidden phrase or title.

408

Find the hidden phrase or title.

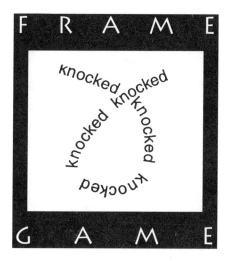

 409

Try your luck at this series. To arrive at each succeeding number, squaring of numbers is required.

0 6 6 20 20 42 42 ?

 410

Given the initial letters of the missing words, complete this sentence.

There are 360 D in a S.

411

Two of the five phrases listed below are equivalent. Which are they?

> **a. 14 square yards**
> **b. 14 yards square**
> **c. 127 square feet**
> **d. 196 square yards**
> **e. 206 yards squared**

 412

Find the hidden phrase or title.

F R A M E

41	end
9	end
13	end
5	end
73	end

G A M E

413

Unscramble the following word:

TESIALLEC

 414

A palindrome is a word or phrase spelled the same both forward and backward, such as noon, dad, deed, and sees. Can you think of three or more palindromic words of at least five letters?

415

In a golf tournament, you're part of the final group on the last day. The first prize is $250,000. One member of the foursome (but not you!) sinks a 50-foot putt on the 72nd hole to win the tournament. You are ecstatic! In fact, that person is the one you hoped would win all along. You didn't have a bet on the outcome, so why are you happy that this golfer won?

416

Change one letter of each succeeding word, starting at the top, to arrive at the word at the bottom.

M E A L

_____

_____

_____

B O O T

417

Find the hidden phrase or title.

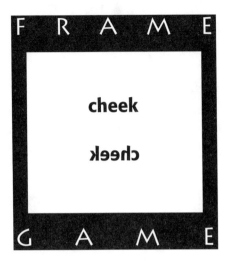

 418

If it were three hours later than it is now, it would be twice as long until midnight as it would be if it were four hours later. What time is it now?

 419

Given the initial letters of the missing words, complete this sentence:

There are 9 P on a B T.

420

Shown below are nine one-inch-long matches. Arrange the matches to create three squares that are the same size.

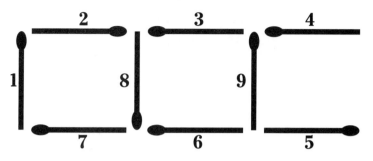

 421

What is the missing number in this series?

Hint: Think of a new approach, rather than going from left to right.

13 4 22 37 44 10 42 ? 15 30 48 39

 422

The meanings of the following five words can change with the addition of a certain common prefix. Can you find that prefix?

stance — station — title — tract — scribe

423

Nancy is Goldie's father's son's wife's daughter. What relation is Goldie to Nancy?

424

Find the hidden phrase or title.

F R A M · E

OINCVS

G A M E

 425

The following is an unusual number series. Don't try to solve it in a normal manner. Take a different route—it might be just a fraction of what you think.

Hint: In any event, don't take longer than a fortnight to solve this.

0 7 1 4 2 8 ?

 **426**

Below is another alphanumeric. Let V = 2 and N = 8.

$$
\begin{array}{r}
\text{FIVE} \\
\text{ONE} \\
\text{ONE} \\
\underline{\text{ONE}} \\
\text{EIGHT}
\end{array}
$$

Find the hidden phrase or title.

Following is the beginning of a word chain. By removing one letter at a time and without rearranging any letters, see if you can come up with a new word on each line.

S T R A I N

_ _ _ _ _

_ _ _ _

_ _ _

_ _

_

429

What are the chances of getting at least two heads when flipping a penny three times?

If you were to lay three identical rectangles on top of each other, what would be the maximum number of resulting intersections? An intersection must be the crossing of two and only two lines; do not include corners. For this puzzle, size the rectangles in a 1:2 proportion. Here's what a start might look like (but it doesn't give us the maximum!):

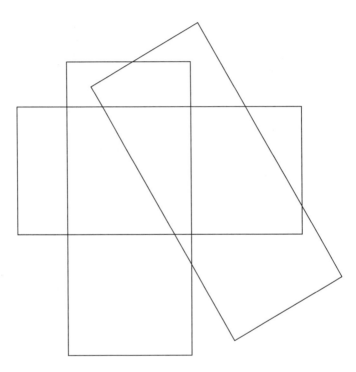

 431

What two numbers will give you an answer of 10 when one is subtracted from the other and an answer of 2,000 when they are multiplied together?

432

Find the hidden phrase or title.

 433

Quickly now, how long is 1,000,000 seconds? Your answer should be in days.

 434

How many digits must be changed in the following addition problem to make the sum 173?

$$
\begin{array}{r}
68 \\
99 \\
+81 \\
\hline
\end{array}
$$

435

Which of the given choices is the next term in this sequence?

PRS, PRT, PRU, PST, PSU, _____

PSV

PSR

PUT

PTU

PUS

 436

Unscramble the following letters to come up with a word that means "puzzle":

E N I T R A E S R A B

437

The numbers in the left-hand column were given the security code numbers in the right-hand column. Can you crack the code to fill in the missing number?

537	**1463**
892	**1108**
1615	**385**
722	**?**

438

What is $\frac{1}{2}$ of $\frac{1}{4}$ of $\frac{2}{9}$ of $\frac{3}{7}$ of 84?

439

In the series 2, 4, 8, 16, 32, 64..., can you come up with a formula using the letter *n* to find the sum of the series, where *n* represents the number of terms in the series?

 440

Imagine a cube 3 × 3 × 3 inches. Now imagine that this cube is divided into 27 one-inch cubes. The maximum number of cubes visible to an observer at any one moment is 19. With a 4 × 4 × 4 cube further subdivided into 64 cubes, the maximum number of cubes that can be seen by an observer at any one moment is 37. How many cubes can be observed in a 5 × 5 × 5 cube (125 smaller cubes total) and a 6 × 6 × 6 cube (216 smaller cubes total)?

441

Below is a spatial/visual analogy.

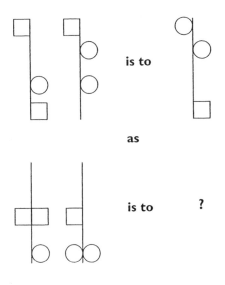

Find the hidden phrase or title.

 443

What comes next in the following sequence?

$$^{1}/_{7} \quad ^{4}/_{9} \quad ^{2}/_{8} \quad ^{5}/_{10} \quad ^{3}/_{9} \quad ^{6}/_{11} \quad ^{?}/_{?}$$

 444

Given the initial letters of the missing words, complete this sentence.

There are 2 P in a Q.

Find the hidden phrase or title.

 446

What conclusion, if any, can you draw from the following?

No humans are not mammals.
No mammals live on Mamal.
Adam Mammale, a former pilot who once lived in Detroit, can live only on Mamal.

447

Change one letter at a time, forming a new word each time, to get from the first word to the last.

P A R T Y

———————

———————

———————

———————

D U N E S

 448

Find the hidden phrase or title.

449

When you decode the message spelled out in the following three triangles, it becomes a riddle. What number answers that riddle?

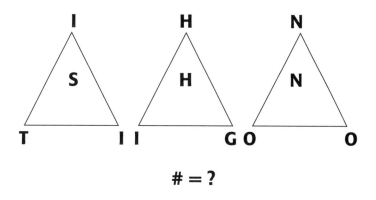

$$\# = ?$$

 450

Here is a number series puzzle that looks complicated but that actually has a very easy solution.

Hint: Only a certain percentage will solve this.

100—100—90—72—50.4—30.24—_____

451

Here is an example of three fractions with the same value that use all the digits from 1 to 9 once and only once:

$$\frac{2}{4} = \frac{3}{6} = \frac{79}{158}$$

Can you find three other such fractions of equal value that use these nine digits only once?

452

Find the hidden phrase or title.

 453

Fill in the letters to complete the following word, which means "fulfilled, achieved."

C O ___ ___ ___ E ___ E ___

454

Here's a different twist on a cube puzzle. The diagram shows six connected squares that need to be folded into a cube. Next to the squares are four views of the same cube. Can you fill in the six squares with the appropriate figures?

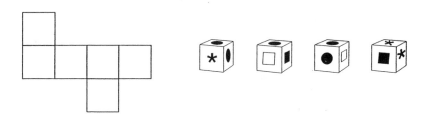

 455

Find the hidden phrase or title.

456

Find the hidden phrase or title.

 457

Chordorfs are less numerous than chlordorfs. Chlorodorfs are more numerous than chlordorfs. Chloroodorfs are less numerous than chlordorfs. If you were to list the most numerous of the preceding four items, from the top down, where would chloroodorfs fit?

 458

Decipher the following cryptogram:

PNOFNO' NO SBT CUNO

459

Find the hidden phrase or title.

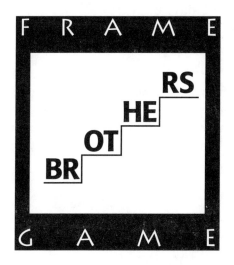

 460

Only one of the fruits listed below is native to North America. Which one?

CRANBERRY—APRICOT—PEAR—

BLACKBERRY—PEACH

 461

Joseph is my uncle's sister's grandaughter's son. What is the closest possible relationship I can have to Joseph?

462

If 30 baseballs are needed for 9 pitchers over 2 days of practice, what is the number of baseballs needed for 11 pitchers over 3 days of practice?

 463

Two of the four cubes pictured below the six connected squares are impossible to make from the six squares. The other two are correct views when the six squares are folded properly into a cube. Which ones are incorrect?

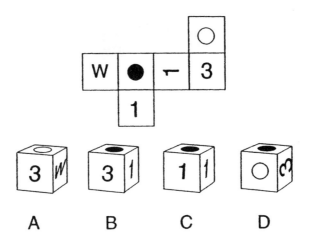

 464

How may words can you find in the word "confession"? (No fair using plurals.)

465

Joe takes three-fifths of a bag of candy. Bob has three-fourths of Pete's share of the remaining candy. What fraction of the total number of pieces of candy does Pete have?

 466

What is the value of F in the following system of equations?

$$A + B = Z \quad (1)$$
$$Z + P = T \quad (2)$$
$$T + A = F \quad (3)$$
$$B + P + F = 30 \quad (4)$$
$$A = 8 \quad (5)$$

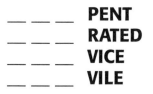 **467**

The following words can all be transformed into new words by prefixing the same three letters, in the same order, at the beginning of the words. What are the three letters?

    _ _ _ **PENT**
    _ _ _ **RATED**
    _ _ _ **VICE**
    _ _ _ **VILE**

468

Can you quickly write down the numbers 1 through 5 so that no two consecutive numbers are next to one another? The first number is not 1, and the second, third, and fourth numbers must increase in value.

469

Below are five squares constructed with toothpicks. Can you move just three toothpicks and come up with four squares—all the same size?

We'll give you one answer, but there's another.

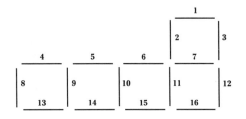

 470

What comes next in this number sequence?

Hint: Get primed for this puzzle.

5   8   26   48   122   ?

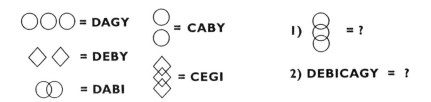 **471**

Determine the relationships between the pictures and the letters to find the solutions:

○○○ = DAGY   ○ over ○ = CABY   1) (picture) = ?

◇ ◇ = DEBY   ◇◇ (stacked) = CEGI   2) DEBICAGY = ?

◎ = DABI

472

Find the hidden phrase or title.

 473

The words *assign* and *stalactite* form a relationship that produces the word *ignite* in parentheses. Can you find a similar relationship between the words *double* and *stationary* that will form a new word in the blank?

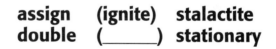

assign   (ignite)   stalactite
double   (_____)   stationary

 474

What is 1,449 in Roman numerals?

475

Here's a balance puzzle. Where does the 25-lb. weight on this teeter-totter go (how many feet from the fulcrum)?

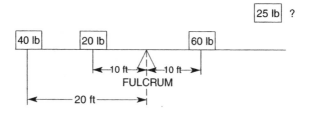

 476

Find the hidden phrase or title.

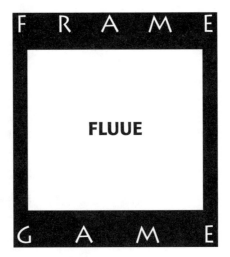

 477

What is $\frac{1}{3}$ divided by $\frac{1}{5}$ divided by $\frac{2}{3}$ times $\frac{3}{5}$?

478

A group of students at a major university was polled to see which courses they were taking. Sixty-four percent were taking English, 22% were taking a foreign language, and 7% were taking both. What percentage of the students polled were taking neither subject?

 479

You need to match three items, A, B, and C, with three numbers, 1, 2, and 3. But you are given some peculiar information by which to determine how to match them up. From the following rules, can you find a solution?

(a) If B is either 2 or 1, then A is 3.
(b) If C is not 2, then A cannot be 3.
(c) If C is not 1, then A is not 3.
(d) If B is 3, then A is not 2.

 480

Here is a five-letter "trickle-down" puzzle. Change one letter at a time to reach the final word.

T I M E R

———————

———————

———————

———————

D U N K S

481

Find the hidden phrase or title.

FRAME

ALL THINGS

all things

GAME

 482

Given the initial letters of the missing words, complete this sentence:

There are 6 O in an I.

 483

Quickly now, solve this puzzle! You are taking a long drink of water. Which happens first?

The glass is $^5/_{16}$ empty.
The glass is $^5/_8$ full.

484

Quickly now, finish this mathematical analogy:

¹/₅ **is to 5 as 5 is to** ___?___ .

 485

Find the hidden phrase or title.

 486

There is a certain logic in the following diagram in the placement of the letters around the triangles. What is the missing letter in the last triangle?

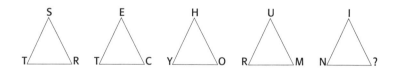

487

Find the hidden phrase or title.

 488

Bill and Tom played several golf matches against each other in a week. They played for a pizza at each match, but no pizzas were purchased until the end of the week. If at any time during the week Tom and Bill had the same number of wins, those pizzas were canceled. Bill won four matches (but no pizzas), and Tom won three pizzas. How many rounds of golf were played?

489

Judy and Mary are Susan's sister's mother-in-law's son's daughters. What relation is Susan to Judy and Mary?

490

Find the hidden phrase or title.

F R A M E

HIS P**ANTS**

G A M E

 491

One way to make eight 8's equal 100 would be as follows:

$$\frac{8888 - 88}{88} = 100$$

Can you devise at least one other way?

 492

How long will it take for you to find three common, everyday words that contain three straight A's? By straight, I mean that they can be separated by consonants, but not by another vowel.

493

Find the hidden phrase or title.

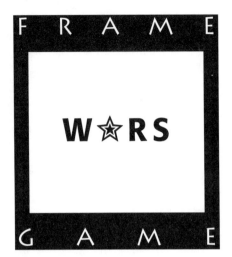

 494

What is the missing number in this grid?

12	27	111
19	39	?
4	9	37

495

A professional bass fisherman caught 30 bass during a five-day tournament. Each day, he caught three more fish than the day before. How many fish did he catch the first day?

496

Given the initial letters of the missing words, complete this phrase:

86,400 S in a D

Hint: You have up to 24 hours to solve this.

 497

Fifteen seconds for this one: Unscramble the following letters to come up with a word game everyone knows.

BLABSCER

 498

How many squares are in the figure below?

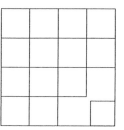

 499

How many numbers are in the following sequence if all terms are included?

0 3 6 9 12 15 18 ... 960

500

Here's an alphametic puzzle that isn't too difficult. See if you can replace the letters with the proper numbers to make this puzzle work.

$$
\begin{array}{r}
\text{HE} \\
\times \text{ME} \\
\hline
\text{BE} \\
\text{Y E} \\
\hline
\text{EWE}
\end{array}
$$

 501

Find the hidden phrase or title.

 502

There are two boxers. The smaller boxer is an amateur and also the son of the bigger boxer, who is a professional. But the pro boxer is not the amateur's father. Who is the pro?

503

Shown below are four ways to divide a four-by-four grid in half. Find the other two ways. No diagonal cuts or rotations allowed (for example, #1 turned 90 degrees doesn't count).

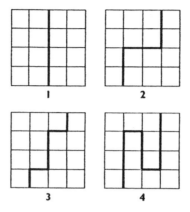

 504

In a game of craps, you are considering betting that the next roll of the dice is going to produce a 2, a 3, or a 12 (not necessarily a come-out roll). A friend who is quick with probabilities advises you against making this bet. Why?

 505

Quickly now, $^1/_7$ is what percentage of $^3/_{11}$?

506

Seven of the following eight words are related. Which is the odd one out and why?

CALCIUM   **IODINE**
IRON   **MAGNESIUM**
PHOSPHORUS   **SELENIUM**
TOCOPHEROL   **ZINC**

 507

Find the hidden phrase or title.

 508

If two-fifths of a fraction is doubled and then multiplied by the original fraction, the result is $1/15$. What is the original fraction (positive numbers only)?

509

A palindromic number is one that reads the same forward and backward, such as 8,315,138. There are only three palindromic squares under 1,000. Two of those are $11^2 =$ 121 and $22^2 = 484$.

What is the third palindromic square under 1,000?
What is the first palindromic square over 1,000?

 510

A little knowledge of algebra may help here. Part of a basketball team stopped by a restaurant and ordered nachos. The bill came to $50.00, but by the time it arrived two of the team members had already left. The remaining members had to pay $1.25 each to cover the bill. How many team members were originally in the restaurant?

 511

How many triangles are in the figure below?

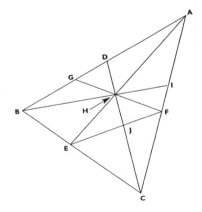

512

Find the hidden phrase or title.

 513

What is the next number in the following sequence?

11 − 23 − 58 − 132 − 134 − 558 − ?

514

From among the integers 1 through 9, can you find six different integers, call them A, B, C, D, E, and F, such that A × B × C = D × E × F?

Hint: Don't use 5 or 7.

515

The letters in several words in the English language lend themselves to being recombined into new words. For example, the word *item* can be transformed into *mite*, and *emit*. The letters of the word *vile* can be rearranged to *live*, *evil*, and *veil*. Try to find a four-letter word that can be changed into four new words (five total, counting your original).

 516

A visitor to a zoo asked the zookeeper how many birds and how many beasts were in a certain section of the zoo. The zookeeper replied: "There are 45 heads and 150 feet, and with that information you should be able to tell me how many of each there are." Can you help the visitor?

 517

Complete the following straightforward math sequence puzzle. It is easier than it appears at first glance.

$$240 - 240 - 120 - 40 - 10 - 2 - \underline{\ ?\ }$$

 518

If 28 equals 24 and 68 equals 76, what does 48 equal?

519

Following is a word written in a code in which each set of two-digit numbers represents a letter. See if you can decipher the word.

41   51   55   55   32   15   44

Hint 1: Notice that 5 is the highest number used.

Hint 2: Think of rows and columns.

 520

In the figure, line **AB** is parallel to line **CD**, angle Y = 50°, and angle Z = 140°. How big is angle X?

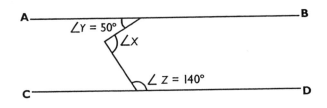

 521

Determine Figure H in the series below.

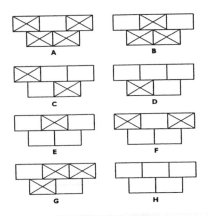

522

The five words listed here share a common trait. By playing with the letters of each word, see if you can determine the trait.

Hint: The same trait is shared with the words apt, tea, and tar.

rifle — evil — deal — rats — tale

 523

One hundred doctors are attending a medical convention. Each doctor is either a surgeon or a dermatologist. At least one is a dermatologist. Given any two of the doctors, at least one is a surgeon. How many are dermatologists and how many are surgeons?

 524

Given the initial letters of the missing words, complete the following sentence. *Hint:* Think of a musical.

76 T led the B P.

 525

Which of the following is larger?

A. $\frac{1}{3}$ times its cube times a dozen cubed
B. $\frac{1}{2}$ times its square times a dozen dozen squared divided by 2 squared times 2 cubed

526

Here's another alphametic:

After seeing what one round of 18 holes of golf would cost at the new country club, Mary decided that today would be an excellent day to play tennis. How much did the round of golf cost (cart included, of course!)?

S E.E S
T E.E S
<u>F E.E S</u>
C A.S H

 527

If two gallons of paint are needed to cover all sides of one cube, how many gallons are needed to cover all exposed surfaces of the figure below? Include surfaces on which the figure is resting. Hint: There are no hidden cubes.

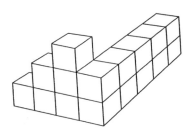

 528

What is the next number in this sequence?

1 4 9 7 7 9 4 1 9 <u>?</u>

529

Find the hidden phrase or title.

 530

What are the values of R and S?

$$Q + M = C$$
$$C + K = R$$
$$R + Q = S$$
$$M + K + S = 40$$
$$Q = 8$$

 531

Decipher the following cryptogram.

AGEGLLGO CM BUGAJNL IBD.

532

Using the number 4 twice and only twice, can you come up with the number 12? You may use any math symbol or sign you wish. Remember, only the number 4 may be used, and only twice.

533

Complete the final wheel:

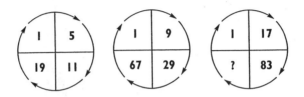

534

Find the hidden phrase or title.

535

What is the next figure in the following series?

 536

One-fifth of a pound of chocolate is balanced perfectly by two-fifths of a block of the same chocolate. What is the weight of the whole block of chocolate?

 537

Find the hidden phrase or title.

538

A man played roulette every day and lost money every day. As the story goes, a fortune teller had put a curse on him that he would lose every time he played roulette. For the ten years since, he has been losing consistently every day, yet he is a very wealthy man who has a loving wife and family. In fact, his wife has even accompanied him daily to the roulette table, where he bets either red or black only. How could this family be so wealthy?

 539

You see here a two-dimensional front view and a two-dimensional top view of a three-dimensional object. Can you sketch what the object looks like in three dimensions?

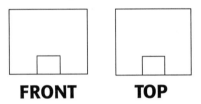

FRONT   **TOP**

 540

What comes next in this sequence?

$$^1/_1 \quad ^9/_8 \quad ^5/_4 \quad ^4/_3 \quad ^3/_2 \quad ^5/_3 \quad ^{15}/_8 \quad ^?/$$

Hint: Think of music.

541

Unscramble the following:

T D I L U E A T

542

Find the hidden phrase or title.

 543

Six hours ago, it was two hours later than three hours before midnight. What time is it?

 544

A jeweler is offering to cut rare gems into fractions to sell to distributors. For $20 a distributor can purchase $1/40$ of an ounce, or for $40 she can purchase $1/20$ of an ounce. Many of the distributors want another cutting in between these two offerings. An enterprising young dealer opens a store across the street and offers $1/30$ of an ounce for $30. Fair enough, right? Where would you buy your gems, or does it even make a difference?

545

What are the next two numbers in the following sequence, and why? (Consider only the first nine numbers.)

8   5   4   9   1   7   6   ?   ?

 546

The box pictured here has been folded together from one of four choices below. Which is the correct one?

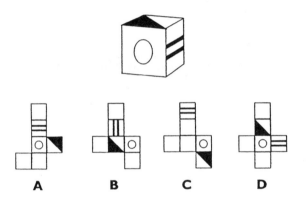

 547

What three-letter word can be added to the beginning of these words to form four new words?

RACKS
FLY
RAGE
BELL

548

Find the hidden phrase or title.

 549

What is the largest sum of money you can have in coins and not be able to make change for a dollar?

 550

Fill in the blank:

Amelia is the daughter of Amanda. Amanda is the _____ of Amelia's mother.

551

Find the hidden phrase or title.

F R A M E

NO ROOM FOR ER

G A M E

 552

If satellite *y* takes three years to make one revolution and satellite *x* takes five years to make one revolution, in how many years will they both be exactly in line and in the same positions as they are now?

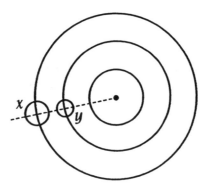

553

Here is a sequence puzzle consisting of the numbers
0 through 9. Complete the sequence by filling in the
remaining numbers. How is the pattern formed?

3   6   9   2   5   8   1   4   ?   ?

 554

Find the hidden phrase or title.

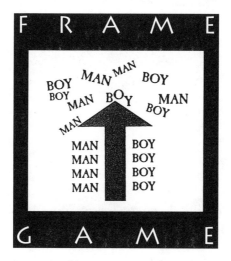

 555

Maria covered the first half of a bicycle race at 20 miles
per hour. The second half of the race was a return over
the same route, and her return speed was 30 miles per
hour. What was Maria's average speed for the entire trip?
Take your time with this.

556

The houses on a street are numbered 1, 2, 3, 4, 5, etc., up one side of the street; then the numbers continue consecutively on the other side of the street and work their way back to be opposite number 1. If house number 12 is opposite house number 29, how many houses are there on both sides of the street?

 557

One of the five following figures does not belong with the rest. Which one is it, and why?

A	B	C	D	E

 558

A boat is coming downstream at 30 mph. On its return, it travels at 10 mph. The trip downstream is three hours shorter than the trip upstream. How far is it from the beginning of the trip to the turnaround point downstream?

 559

If Alicia is three times as old as Amy will be when Alex is as old as Alicia is now and Alex's age is a square number, who is the second oldest? Can you give their ages now?

560

What 12-letter word is written in the block below? Start with any letter and move one letter at a time, in any direction, but don't go back over any letter!

O	I	R	T
G	N	E	T
O	M	R	Y

 561

Fill in the two missing numbers in the following boxes.

Hint: Think outside the boxes.

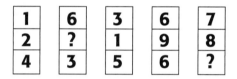

 562

A certain pipe can fill a swimming pool in two hours; another pipe can fill it in five hours; a third pipe can empty the pool in six hours. With all three pipes turned on exactly at the same time, and starting with an empty pool, how long will it take to fill the pool?

 563

Can you find 50 different words in the word "arithmetic"?

564

Given the initial letters of the missing words, complete this sentence.

There are 5 S to a P.

 565

Find the hidden phrase or title.

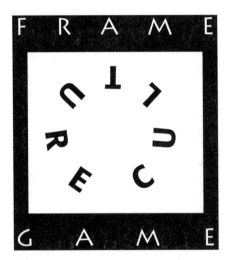

 566

The proportion of southpaws among pitchers is greater than among players in general. Is there a statement that can be made for certain about the proportion of pitchers among left-handers compared to all ballplayers? Is it greater, smaller, or the same, or is there not enough information to tell?

567

Can you discover what is going on in the following figures? What is the relationship among the circles, squares, and dividing line that determines the respective numbers? What number goes with the sixth figure?

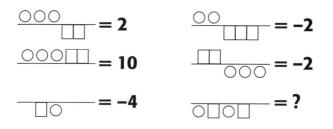

 568

Find the hidden phrase or title.

569

What is the next number in this sequence?

5   6   8   7   9   3   4   5   10   2   11   ?

 570

Draw a square. Now divide the square into four equal, congruent parts with three straight lines. None of the lines may cross each other within the square.

 571

Find the hidden phrase or title.

572

Change the position of one match stick to correct the following equation.

Hint: Think Roman.

 573

Quickly now, which of the following symbols denotes mercury in the periodic table of the elements?

Me Mr Hg Hr My

 574

At a reception, one-third of the guests departed at a certain time. Later, two-fifths of the remaining guests departed. Even later, two-thirds of those guests departed. If six people were left, how many were originally at the party?

575

Here is a word that needs to be unscrambled into an ordinary word recognizable to most anyone:

CRICKARFREE

576

Find the hidden phrase or title.

F R A M E

Party GATE

G A M E

 577

Move from the first word to the last in six moves, changing one letter each time to form a new word.

T R E A T

———

———

———

———

B L O O D

The dreaded cube-eaters from the fourth dimension descend upon a stack of 27 identical sugar cubes. Cube-eaters can only eat to the center of a cube. When they reach the center, they always make a 90° turn and proceed to the next cube. They never reenter a cube. If a cube-eater enters at location A, what is the minimum number of cubes it will eat through to reach the cube at location B?

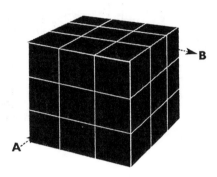

 579

Here is a list of scores from a fictitious college football season. Based on the given scores only, see if you can figure out who would win and by how much if Harvard were to play Montana during this season.

Montana 27	**Notre Dame 13**
Harvard 17	**New Hampshire 16**
Notre Dame 14	**Ohio State 10**
New Hampshire 24	**Connecticut 21**
Ohio State 10	**BYU 7**
Connecticut 28	**Maine 24**
Maine 35	**BYU 3**

580

How many individual cubes are in this stack of cubes? Assume that all rows and columns are complete unless you actually see them end.

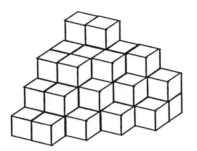

 581

Find the hidden phrase or title.

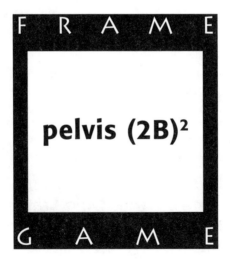

582

Five types of flowers grow in five gardens on five different streets. Given the following information, determine which flowers grow where.

1. The Smiths do not grow violets.
2. The Morgans grow peonies; they do not live on 2nd Street.
3. The Parks live on 3rd Street.
4. Begonias bloom on 4th Street.
5. Roses do not grow on 5th Street.
6. The Johnsons do not live on 1st Street.
7. The Rosens do not grow daffodils.
8. The Johnsons grow roses.
9. Daffodils grow on 1st Street.

 583

What is the missing number in this sequence?

$$(7, 8) \quad (19, 27) \quad (37, 64) \quad (61, 125)$$
$$(91, 216) \quad (?, 343)$$

 584

You have the four kings and four queens from a deck of cards. Place the queens on top of the kings facedown in one stack. Pick up the stack, and starting with the top card (queen), place it faceup on a table. Take the second card and place it facedown on the bottom of the cards in your hand; place the third card faceup on the table, the fourth card on the bottom, and so on, until all cards are faceup. What is the order of the cards that are faceup?

585

Find the hidden phrase or title.

 586

Given the initial letters of the missing words, complete this sentence.

There are 14 D in a F.

 587

See if you can unscramble the following words to make a sensible sentence out of them.

Last they say who best laughs or, he laughs so.

588

Here's another "trickle-down" puzzle. Change one letter on each line to reach the final word. There may be more than one way to do this puzzle.

P E S T

———————

———————

———————

B A T S

 589

Find the hidden phrase or title.

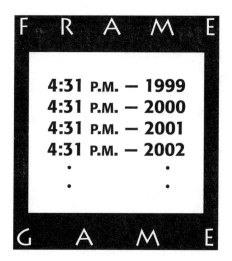

Below are three intersecting circles that have a maximum of seven bounded areas that are not further subdivided. What is the maximum number of bounded areas that result when six circles are intersected?

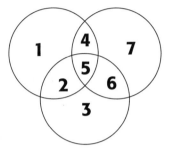

 591

Here is a form of syllogism. Assume that the first three statements are true and then determine whether the fourth statement, the conclusion, is valid or false. That's all there is to it!

Some *zers* are *tifs*.
All *tifs* are *xorts*.
Some *xorts* are *wols*.
Therefore, some *zers* are definitely *wols*.

 592

In Puzzle 214 you were asked to come up with as many ten-letter words as you could using only the letter keys from the top row of a typewriter. Those letters are: Q, W, E, R, T, Y, U, I, O, and P. The classic solution to that puzzle is the word TYPEWRITER. Of course, there are others.

Here's a new twist. Can you make at least one nine-letter word from those same letters? You may use any of the letters more than once.

593

Find the hidden phrase or title.

F R A M E

M☆KING

G A M E

 594

If 14 equals 12 and 34 equals 38, what does 24 equal?

 595

What follows is an argument: a premise and a conclusion based on that premise. See if you can determine whether the argument is valid or invalid.

> If we are to survive and prosper as a species, solving the riddles of the universe via mathematics becomes the single most important focus of theoreticians. Thus, only the most brilliant minds will succeed.

596

Unscramble these letters to make a word:

RALLEAPL

 597

One glass is one-sixth full of blue liquid dye. Another glass, exactly the same size, is one-seventh full of the blue dye. Each glass is then filled to the top with water and their contents mixed together in a large container. What proportion of this final mixture is blue dye and what proportion is water?

 598

Find the hidden phrase or title.

One of the figures shown here lacks a characteristic common to the other five. Which figure is it, and why?

Hint: Don't consider symmetry.

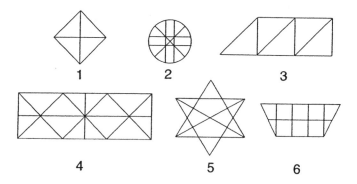

 600

Find the hidden phrase or title.

601

A ten-letter word is hidden here. The last letter, R, is placed outside the grid of the other letters. Using each letter only once, and beginning with the first letter of the word, which may be in any of the nine positions of the grid, spell the word by moving up, down, sideways, or diagonally to adjacent letters.

```
        A   L   C
    R   O   C   U
        T   A   L
```

 602

Find the hidden phrase or title.

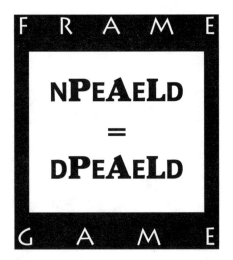

603

In the following puzzle, the first number in each box has a certain relationship with the second number in that box. The relationships are the same for all four boxes. What is the missing number?

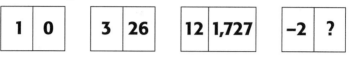

| 1 | 0 | | 3 | 26 | | 12 | 1,727 | | –2 | ? |

 604

This next sequence puzzle is math related, but not exactly what you might think at first. Fill in the missing term.

Hint 1: Think leap year.

Hint 2: Be careful! Some calculators will give you the wrong answer.

$$0-3-4-4-8-2-\underline{}$$

 605

Here's a somewhat different perspective on the counting of stacked cubes. How many total cubes are there? Assume that all rows and columns are complete unless you actually see them end.

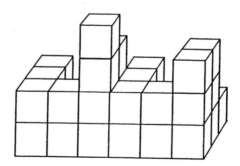

Four married couples live on a street in four different-colored houses. Given the information below, can you determine who is married to whom and the color of their house? (One of the houses is red.)

1. Harry does not live in the white house.
2. Alice is not married to Brad.
3. Steve lives in the yellow house.
4. John is not married to June.
5. Harry does not live in the blue house.
6. Alice lives in the blue house.
7. June is married to Harry.
8. Nancy is not married to Steve.
9. Sara is one of the wives.

607

Find the hidden phrase or title.

608

Given the following letters and numbers, come up with the correct phrase:

There are 24 K in P G.

 609

All the words listed below share a common theme. What is it?

Timer
Spool
Reward
Emit
Diaper
Desserts

 610

See if you can ascertain the nature of the relationship among the pictures in each row in order to fill in the missing figure in row 3.

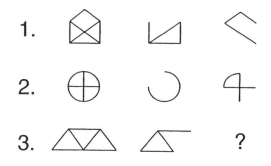

611

Find the hidden phrase or title.

FRAME

DNIMIND

GAME

 612

I am six times as old as my sister. In one year I will be five times as old as my sister will be. In six years I will be three times as old as my sister will be. How old am I and how old is my sister?

 613

The three words on the left have an interesting characteristic that is reversed with the three words on the right. Can you identify what that characteristic (and its reverse) is?

federal	defy
pond	hijack
ruts	calmness

614

Sometimes people wonder whether puzzles have any real-life applications. You be the judge. Here's an example:

A mother was throwing a birthday party for her daughter and realized that, with only nine scoops of ice cream, there wasn't enough to give two scoops to each of the five children present. She quickly came up with an idea that pleased all—and everyone got an equal amount of ice cream. By the way, she did not divide the scoops into fractional portions. How did this real-life mom solve her dilemma?

 615

Here is another *alphametic*: Fred, a football fanatic, is going to his first University of Nebraska football game. He doesn't know that Nebraska has the nation's longest streak of consecutive sellouts for their home games. See if you can find the number of people that were sitting in the north end zone with Fred. Each letter in the following alphametic retains the same value within the problem, and the value must be different from that of any other letter. Zero may not begin a word.

$$
\begin{array}{r}
\mathbf{RED} \\
\mathbf{RED} \\
\mathbf{RED} \\
+\mathbf{FRED} \\
\hline
\mathbf{HORDE}
\end{array}
$$

616

Find the hidden phrase or title.

 617

Here are five words. The first four are newly created English words that are related to their respective patterns. For the fifth pattern, you have to come up with the word; for the last word, you have to come up with the pattern.

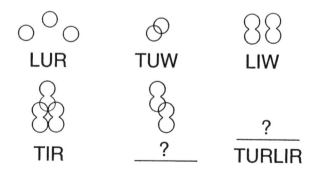

618

You are playing a game with a friend called "penny pickup" in which nine pennies are placed on a table. In alternating turns, each player picks up at least one, but not more than five pennies per turn. The player who picks up the last penny wins. However, the penny has to be the only one left for that player to win. In other words, if your opponent picks up five pennies, you can't pick up four and call yourself the winner. Under these guidelines, if you go first, is there a move you can make to ensure that you win?

 619

Find the hidden phrase or title.

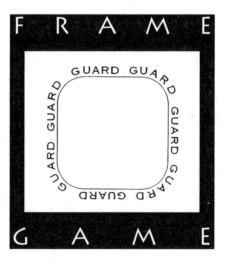

 620

A zookeeper has to put 27 snakes in four cages. His problem is that he must have an odd number of snakes in each cage. How can he accomplish this? You can put any number of snakes in a cage as long as the total number of snakes in each cage is an odd number.

621

At a convention of baseball trading card collectors, 30 dealers are interested in trading or selling their extra Mickey Mantle cards. Fifteen of the dealers have fewer than five such cards to trade, 11 others have more than six of them to trade, and three others have more than seven to trade or sell. What is the total number of dealers that have five, six, or seven Mickey Mantle cards?

 622

Here is a series challenge for the better brainteaser fan. Fill in the missing term in this mathematical series.

9–73–241–561–1,081–1,849–?

 623

Given the following letters and numbers, come up with the correct phrase.

Hint: This is not a particularly common phrase, but it's solvable. Think "game."

225 S on a S B

 624

What is the next letter in the following odd sequence?

O–T–F–S–N–E–___

625

In five minutes, how many words can you make out of the word **crazed** (any number of letters allowed)?

626

Find the hidden phrase or title.

 627

Bob was paddling his canoe upstream at a constant rate. After six miles, the wind blew his hat into the stream. Thinking that he had no chance to recover his hat, he continued upstream for six more miles before turning back. He continued rowing at the same rate on his return trip and overtook his hat at exactly the same spot where he began his journey, eight hours earlier. What was the velocity of the stream?

 628

What letter comes next in the following sequence?
   Hint: Go straight to the answer.

A—E—F—H—I—K—L—M—N—___

629

What is the fewest number of lines that would need to be erased to do away with all of the triangles in this figure?

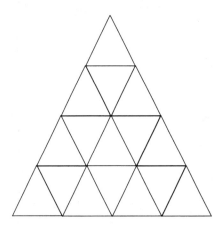

 630

A traveler at an airport had lots of time to kill between flights, so he decided to conduct an experiment on one of the moving walkways. He found he could walk the length of the walkway, moving in its forward direction, in one minute. Walking at the same rate *against* the forward direction of the walkway, it took him three minutes to cover the same distance. He wondered how long it would take him to cover one length if the walkway were to stop. Can you help him out? (This may not be as easy as it first appears.)

631

Find the hidden phrase or title.

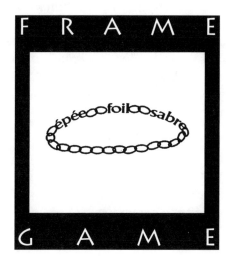

 632

Which one of the following patterns does not belong with the rest?

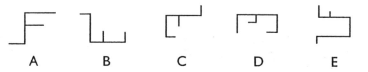

A B C D E

 633

Unscramble the following:

CITURSIUFT

634

Using three nines, what is the largest number that can be created? You may use any mathematical symbols or signs you wish, with the exception of infinity (∞) and ellipses (…). You may not use any of the three nines together in combination, such as 99 × 9. In other words, each nine must remain by itself before any math operation is performed on it. Additionally, no mathematical symbol or sign may be used more than four times.

 635

Find the hidden phrase or title.

 636

The following is in code. Can you crack the code and decipher the message?

JZF'CP LD JZFYR LD JZF QPPW.

637

A box of candy can be divided equally among three, five, or thirteen people. What is the smallest number of pieces of candy the box can contain?

 638

What 9-letter word is written in the block below? Start with any letter and move one letter at a time, in any direction, but don't go back over any letter!

O N N
C U D
M U R

 639

The six words listed here share a common trait. What is it?

pride—slime—grant—price—globe—whole

 640

Unscramble these letters to make a word.

YONNMSY

 641

What is the missing number in the following series?
Hint: Tackling this puzzle head-on won't help you. Try different directions.

23—48—9—39— ? —51—12—37

Try your luck at this "trickle-down" puzzle. Remember, change one letter at a time to arrive at the answer.

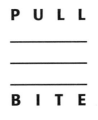

P U L L

——————

——————

——————

B I T E

 643

Find the hidden phrase or title.

 644

Find the missing number in the following series:

3   3   10   11   21   23   ?

ANSWERS

1. Construct a chart to consider the possible values.

E	1	2	3	4	5	6	7	8	9
Carryovers			1	1	2	2	2	3	3
N	4	8	2	6	0	4	8	2	6
4N + Carryovers	6	2	9	5	2	8	4	1	7

E cannot equal zero since that would make N zero. We need a value where four E's equal N and four N's are equal to E plus a carryover. From the chart, we see that the only place where that occurs is when E equals 2. Therefore, E = 2, N = 8, and O must equal 1, since any number greater than that would result in an additional carryover.

$$
\begin{array}{r}
182 \\
182 \\
182 \\
+182 \\
\hline
728
\end{array}
$$

2. When referring to columns, they are numbered from left to right. In the first column, N + M + S is equal to a number less than 10. Therefore, the greatest number of the three could be a 6 with no carryover from the second column, or a 5 with a carryover from the second column. Obviously, there is a carryover from, or to, at least one of the two middle columns, since their sums yield two different letters.

Let's make an assumption that there is a carryover to the first column, and, therefore, no number can be greater than 5 in that column.

Now consider the possibilities for the last column.

N	1	2	3	4	5
Carryovers				1	1
E	3	6	9	2	5

N cannot equal 5, because then E would equal 5. If N = 1, O would have to be 7, which is impossible, since the sum of the second column would then be 23. If N = 3, then O = 1 and U must also be 3, which is impossible. N cannot equal 4 because that would mean that O would equal 1, and both remaining numbers in the first column would be greater than 4. Therefore, N equals 2 and E equals 6.

If N is 2, then O must be 4. Since we accounted for the numbers 2, 3, and 4, M + S can only equal 1 and 5, and they are interchangeable.

2442   2442
5442   1442
+1442   +5442
9326   9326

3. Here are three solutions. Can you find others?

8026   8096   8069
26   96   96
938   748   758
+1280   +1980   1980
_____   _____   _____
10270   10920   10930

4. Since A + B = Z and Z + P = T, it follows that A + B + P = T. We also know that T + A = F, so adding the last two equations and simplifying, we get 2A + B + P = F. We know that B + P + F = 24, so we have:

$$24 - B - P = F$$
$$\underline{2A + B + P = F}$$
$$24 + 2A = 2F \text{ or } 12 + A = F$$

We can replace F with T + A. The equation then becomes 12 + A = T + A, so T = 12 and therefore Q = 19.

5. View C is not correct.

6. Besides the three shown in this puzzle, eight other ways are possible.

7. It is always helpful to set up a legend of what is given and to work from there.

$$X = \$.50 \text{ pens}$$
$$Y = \$5.50 \text{ pens}$$
$$Z = \$9.50 \text{ pens}$$

Set up two equations as follows:

$$X + Y + Z = 100$$
$$\$.50X + \$5.50Y + \$9.50Z = 100$$

Now, we need at least one of the values to drop out in order to consider the other two. Multiply the first equation by − .5 to drop X out of both equations.

$$
\begin{array}{r}
- 0.5X \;\; - 0.5Y \;\; - 0.5Z = -50 \\
+ 0.5X \;\; + 5.5Y \;\; + 9.5Z = 100 \\
\hline
+ 5.0Y \;\; + 9.0Z = \;\; 50
\end{array}
$$

$$5Y = 50 - 9Z$$
$$Y = 10 - Z$$

Since we're dealing with whole numbers, Z must be a whole number and a multiple of 5. In this case, Z can only equal 5. With any greater number, Y will become a negative number. So, Z = 5 and Y becomes 1, leaving X to be 94 pens at $.50.

$$94 \text{ pens at } \$.50$$
$$1 \text{ pen at } \$5.50$$
$$5 \text{ pens at } \$9.50$$

8. B, C, and D form the triangle.

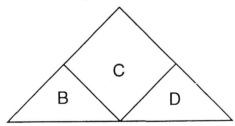

9. Q, K, Q, Q, K, K, and K is the order that works.

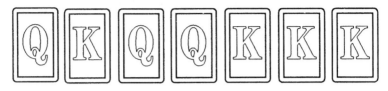

10.

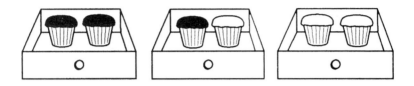

As you can see, there are only three possibilities where a chocolate cupcake could be chosen first.

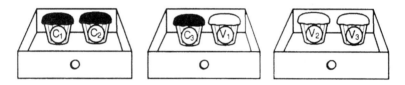

Out of these three, there are only two where a chocolate cupcake could be chosen second.

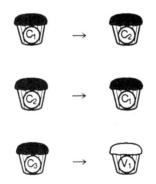

The answer is two out of three.

11. If the first digit of the four-digit code cannot be 0, 5, or 7, that leaves seven possible numbers for the first digit. All ten digits, however, can be used for the second, third, and fourth numbers.

$$7 \times 10 \times 10 \times 10$$

There are 7,000 possible different code words.

12. Columns are numbered from left to right. There has to be a carry-over of 2 to the first column. If P were 9 and Q were 8, with a carry-over of 1 from the last column, the sum of 20 could not be reached if R equaled 1. Therefore, R cannot be 1.

13. The powers of 7 have a repeating pattern for the last digit that can be found easily without performing the entire multiplication of each power.

$$7^0 \quad 7^1 \quad 7^2 \quad 7^3 \quad 7^4 \quad 7^5 \quad 7^6 \quad 7^7$$
$$1 \quad 7 \quad 9 \quad 3 \quad 1 \quad 7 \quad 9 \quad 3$$

With a repeating pattern of four, 7^{32} has the same remainder as 7^0, which is 1. Then 7^{33} would be in the next column, 7^1. Its remainder is 7 when divided by 10.

14. This type of puzzle is a form of syllogism. It can best be shown by using Venn diagrams.

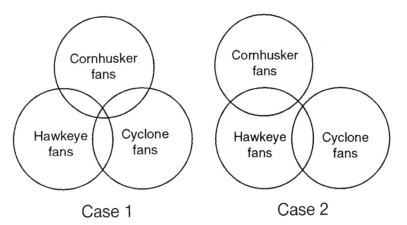

Case 1   Case 2

From Case 1, we can see that it is possible for a Cornhusker to be a Cyclone fan, but from Case 2, it is not definite. The conclusion is false.

15. Obviously, their number system is based on something other than 10. Let's say it is based on a notation represented by N.

3N + 0, their number 30, is the number we call 24.

You can reason that 3N + 0 = 24, and N = 8.

Likewise, 3N + 4 = 28, and N = 8.

Their number system is then BASE$_8$ and $5 \times 4 \times 7$, our 140, becomes their 214.

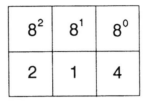

8^2	8^1	8^0
2	1	4

16. Since Dave spoke to the biologist, and Ann was sitting next to the chemist and across from the doctor, Cathy must be the author, and Ann is the biologist. The doctor didn't speak, but Dave did. So, Boobie is the doctor (and was thinking of her own parents) and Dave is the chemist.

17. Turn the first grid 90° to the right, and delete the bottom row of figures. Then turn the result 90° to the right again and delete the

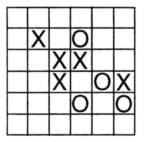

bottom row. Do the same with the third grid to get the answer.

18. The sum is ⅓. Can you determine what the sum is of the infinite series ⅓ + ⅑ + ¹⁄₂₇ + ¹⁄₈₁ . . . ?

19. You can approach this puzzle in several ways.

REBRAG =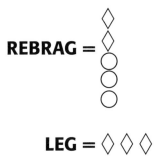

LEG = ◇ ◇ ◇

One of the first things you may have noticed is that the horizontal figures both contain an L, whereas the two vertical figures contain an R. The equations with two figures both contain a B and the equations with three figures both have a G. The circles have an A and the diamonds an E for their lone vowels. So, that yields this basic information.

L = horizontal	**B = 2**
R = vertical	**A =** ◯
G = 3	**E =** ◇

20. In the first two foreign phrases, roi is the only common word. The word "three" in the English version is likewise the only common word; so, roi means "three." In the second and third foreign phrases, the word kir is used. The English translations share the word meaning "coins." So, kir means coins. Comparing the first and third phrases, we see they share the word kaf, meaning "take." Therefore, kaf means "take." From the English translation of the first phrase, "Kaf navcki roi," we know that navcki means "pieces." From the second phrase, palt must mean "hide," and from the third phrase, inoti means "cautiously."

"Hide pieces cautiously" becomes "Palt navcki inoti," assuming that the foreign syntax follows that of English.

21. The probability is 14.3 percent. Twenty-two percent of the people are not gum chewers and 65 percent are over fifteen years old. Therefore, 22 percent $\times$ 65 percent or 14.3 percent are not gum chewers and are above the age of fifteen.

22. The only relationship these capital letters have is that their shapes are totally or partially closed. R is the next and last letter of the alphabet that meets this requirement.

23. The answer is "A is larger than B by 1." This is a good example of reducing a seemingly difficult problem to an example that is workable.

For instance, $2^5 = 32$.
$2^4(16) + 2^3(8) + 2^2(4) + 2^1(2) + 2^0(1) = 31$
That is 1 less than 32.

24. It only took John four steps to accomplish his task.
  Step 1—John filled the five-gallon bucket and poured all of it into the six-gallon bucket.
  Step 2—He refilled the five-gallon bucket and poured out one gallon into the six-gallon bucket to fill it, leaving four gallons in the five-gallon bucket.
  Step 3—He dumped the six-gallon bucket and poured the four gallons from the five-gallon bucket into the six-gallon bucket.
  Step 4—Then, John refilled the five-gallon bucket and started home for a piece of cake.

25. The answer is 6119. These four numbers read the same right side up as they do upside down. The numbers on the right are the ones that most closely follow the ones on the left.

26. EMIT spelled backwards is TIME. STAR spelled backwards is RATS.

27. The next number is 4. Here's how to set up the problem.

If the difference of the numbers of the series is taken to the end, a pattern of –3 is established. The next number in the series must yield a –3 in the bottom row. The number next to –8 must be –11. Next to –6 is a –17, and 4 is next to 21.

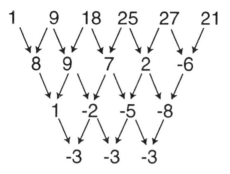

So, here's how we complete the diagram of the setup.

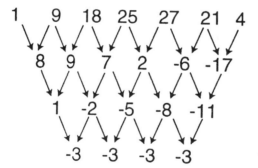

28. In one day, nine men work at a rate of X compared to seven women who work at a rate of Y. This can be expressed as:

$$9X + 7Y =$$

Likewise in the second case:

$$7X + 11Y =$$

Taking these two equations together, we have:

$$9X + 7Y =$$
$$7X + 11Y =$$

$$45X + 35Y = 1$$
$$28X + 44Y = 1$$

$$45X + 35Y = 28X + 44Y$$
$$17X = 9Y$$

$$\frac{\text{Y or women's rate}}{\text{X or men's rate}} = \frac{17}{9}$$

The women are better workers by a ratio of 17 to 9.

29. The next number is 224. Notice that no digit is greater than 4. That's because these are the BASE_{10} numbers 1, 2, 4, 8, 16, 32, and 64 converted to numbers in BASE_5.

30. The missing number is 1. This is the fraction $^1/_7$ converted to decimal form.

31. The number is 8. Starting with the first and last numbers and working towards the middle, each pair of numbers totals 20.

32. The next number is 30. This is actually two different series contained within one. One series begins with 0 and continues with every other number. Likewise, starting with the 2, a second series is established with every other number.

33. The missing number is 5. Each number stands for a letter of the alphabet where A = 1, B = 2, C = 3, etc. The word spelled out is PUZZLES.

34. The answer is 51. In this problem, the differences between the numbers forms a pattern, allowing you to predict the next numbers. After finding the difference, find the difference of the resulting numbers.

35. The correct number is 51. These numbers represent the answers for each of the six problems starting with Puzzle 29.

36. Unscrambled, the letters spell out ALBERT EINSTEIN.

37. The maximum number of cubes is nineteen.

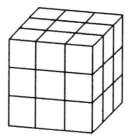

38. There are several different methods of approaching this problem. Since there are three unknowns, it is helpful to establish whatever relationship may exist between the unknowns and then attempt to express that relationship in common terms.

Looking at the first two parts of the equations, we see that § = 2⊗.

We know that ¶ − § = 6 and, therefore, § = ¶ − 6, which means that 2⊗ = ¶ − 6.

If we replace each § with 2⊗, we then have 7⊗ = 2¶.

Solving for ⊗ in the third equation, we have $⊗ = \dfrac{¶ - 6}{2}$.

Solving for ⊗ in the fourth equation, we have $⊗ = \dfrac{2¶}{7}$.

$$\dfrac{¶ - 6}{2} = \dfrac{2}{7} \qquad 3¶ = 42$$
$$7(¶ - 6) = 4¶ \qquad ¶ = 14$$
$$7¶ - 42 = 4¶ \qquad § = 8$$
$$ \qquad ⊗ = 4$$

39. Each X moves clockwise on the outside squares. Each O moves counterclockwise.

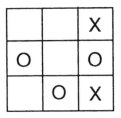

40. From several thousand feet high, the pyramid would look like this. The 60° angle between Lines A and B would appear to be 90° to Judy.

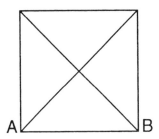

41. Rendrag paid $120 for the entire trip, so for the half of the trip the students were traveling, Rendrag paid $60.00. For the price to be mathematically equitable, the students would each pay $20 to Rendrag for a total of $40. Rendrag's portion for this part of the trip is $20 also.

42. Think of the two figures as an opaque rectangle that has an opaque square behind it. To arrive at the second part of the analogy, the square (the bottom figure) rotates 45° in either direction, and the rectangle (the top figure) rotates 90° in either direction.

To find the correct solution, rotate the rectangle (now the bottom figure) 45°, and rotate the square (now the top figure) 90°. The answer is C.

43. Consider the first figure in the analogy to be two transparent triangles sharing a common base. Let the triangle on the left flip downwards, using the base as an axis. This will give you the second figure. Likewise, in the third figure, let the line connected to the circle on the left fall around the base. C is the answer.

44. A cube is made up of six planes; a tetrahedron has four planes. A triangle has three planes, so it needs two lines to keep it in the same 6 to 4 (3 to 2) ratio. Only A works.

45. In the first two figures of the analogy, place the vertical line of the second figure directly behind the vertical line of the first. Where two flags meet on the same side of the line, they turn into a square on the third figure. Where a flag and a circle meet, they cancel each other out, and no figure appears. If flags or circles are unopposed, they appear as they are on their respective sides of the combined lines. The result is:

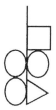

46. C is the only figure that can't be completed with one continuous line that does not retrace any part of the figure.

47. Think it's impossible? It can be done.

The northbound train pulls into the siding, leaving its tail end hanging out on the main track. Meanwhile, the southbound train stays beyond the north switch of the siding, on the main track. When the northbound train stops just short of Point Z (in railroad terms, "in the clear of the main track"), the crew signals the southbound train to proceed south on the main track.

After the southbound train has pulled down fifty or sixty cars, it stops. At Point Z, one of its crew members makes a cut on the fifty or so cars of the southbound train. The southbound train pulls far enough down the main track to allow the northbound train to get out of the siding. The southbound train will have enough room to pull down and not interfere with the cars from the northbound train that are still on the main track.

The crew from the northbound train lines the switch at the top end of the siding, and the northbound train proceeds north, coupling its engine onto the remaining cars of the southbound train. It shoves north, leaving the siding completely. A member of the southbound train's crew lines the bottom end of the siding switch for the main track, and the southbound train pulls its car down two miles or so and stops. Another crew member lines the switch at the top end of the siding for the main track.

The northbound train proceeds south. The engine is pushing its 100 cars and pulling the remaining cars from the southbound train. When the northbound train (now traveling south) gets all its cars past the bottom or southern end of the siding, it lines the siding switch and shoves the remaining cars from the southbound train into the siding. When it comes back out, a crew member lines the switch for the main track, and the train proceeds north with its entire train intact.

The southbound train shoves back to the siding, picks up its remaining cars, and heads south with its entire train. (Hopefully, the crew of the southbound train will line the bottom siding switch for the main track after they pull out, so the next train won't have an open siding switch to worry about.)

48. Border patrol

49. Good with numbers

50. Since Gear R has to make a complete trip around both fixed gears, it doesn't make any difference where we begin. For clarity's sake, we'll start as shown here.

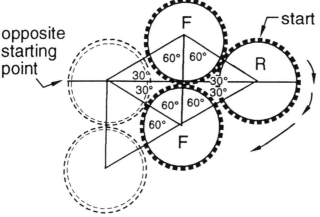

Keep in mind that if Gear R were to revolve around only the top fixed gear, it would make two revolutions, since their diameters are the same. Therefore, Gear R will make one revolution when it reaches the position of the lower left dashed circle.

In order for Gear R to continue to a position opposite its starting point, it needs to travel 60° more, as shown. Since 60°/180° = $\frac{1}{3}$, Gear R makes an additional $\frac{1}{3}$ revolution, for a total of $1\frac{1}{3}$ revolutions to its halfway point. Multiply that by 2 for the whole rotation, and you find that the answer is $2\frac{2}{3}$ revolutions.

51. The question asks for rates. These are usually expressed in units of time, in this case, miles per hour (m.p.h.). We are not really interested in the fact that Sara may have traveled two or more hours, because her rate will always be the same.

In one hour, Sara will travel 4 miles down the river. Coming back, against the current, she must travel the same 4 miles, but it will take her two hours to accomplish this. In order to get a rate for one hour, we have to find out how far she traveled against the current in one hour, and that is 2 miles.

Sara travels a total of 6 miles in two hours for a rate of 3 m.p.h. Since she has gone up and down the river, the rate of the river is cancelled out, and Sara's rate is 3 m.p.h. (6 miles divided by two hours) in still water, which means the rate of the river is 1 m.p.h.

52. Candace is Jane's niece.

53. In a twelve-hour period starting after either 6 a.m. or 6 p.m., there will be eleven times when the hands are directly opposite each other. Twelve hours divided by eleven equals 1 hour, 5 minutes, and $27\frac{3}{11}$ seconds. Go back the 1 hour, 5 minutes, and $27\frac{3}{11}$ seconds from 6 o'clock, and you get 4:54 and $32\frac{8}{11}$ seconds.

54. The missing letter is R. The letters spell out "What is the answer?"

55. The sum of the three numbers below the diameter equals $\frac{1}{3}$ of the top number. So, the answer is one.

56. Ten weights will balance either 50 gold coins or 40 silver coins. Since only 20 gold coins are used, that means the weight of 30 gold coins is to be used by the silver coins. The weights are in a 4-to-5 ratio, and ⁴/₅ of 30 = 24. So, 24 silver coins should be added to the 20 gold coins to balance the 10 weights.

57. Here are the answers.

$$A = 3$$
$$B = 1$$
$$C = 4$$
$$D = 2$$

58. The 2-inch hose will drain the water faster, since it has a bigger spout area than the two 1-inch hoses. The area of a circle is given by multiplying π(3.14) times the radius squared. The radius of the 2-inch hose is 1 inch. Its area is equal to $\pi \times 1 \times 1$ or π square inches. The area of the two 1-inch hoses is:

$$\pi \times \tfrac{1}{2} \times \tfrac{1}{2} + \pi \times \tfrac{1}{2} \times \tfrac{1}{2}$$

or $\frac{\pi}{4} + \frac{\pi}{4}$, which equals $\frac{\pi}{2}$ square inches

The 2-inch hose drains water twice as fast.

59.

$$41067$$
$$\underline{41607}$$
$$\$826743$$

60.

6	2174
+ 6	2980
12	5154

61. The numbers are the numbers on the telephone, as shown here.

ABC	DEF	GHI	JKL	MNO	PRS	TUV	WXY
2	3	4	5	6	7	8	9

If the number is slanted to the left, then the left-most letter of that grouping is the letter to be used. If it is slanted to the right, the right-most letter is the choice. Letters that are straight up and down are represented by the center letter.

The note says, "Went to buy a new phone."

62. If 81 students had taken a course in geography, then only 9 students out of the 90 (10 took neither) took only geology. Since 63 students out of 90 had taken geology, that leaves 27 who had taken only geography.

$$27 + 9 = 36 \qquad\qquad {}^{36}/_{100} \text{ is 36 percent}$$

The answer is 36 percent or nine out of twenty-five.

Since 36 students took either geography or geology and 10 took neither, that leaves 54 percent who took at least one class in both.

63. Unfinished Symphony

64. Although the chances are remote, you just might pull the 24 blue socks out first. You'd need two more to make certain to get two black socks. You'd be assured of a pair of black socks by pulling 26 socks.

65. The first two digits enclosed within any parentheses are added together to get the second number contained within each parentheses. To get the first two digits of any following parentheses, add the numbers found in the preceding parentheses together. In this case, that is:

37:10

66. Dashing through the snow.

67. Let's take a look at how this might be accomplished. Each letter represents a different person present at the gathering. Remember that when one person shakes another's hand, each person gets credit for a handshake. There are several ways to accomplish this. Here's one.

> X shakes hands with W, Y, Z, T.
> Y shakes hands with W, Z, T, X.
> W shakes hands with Z, T, X, Y.
> Z shakes hands with R, X, Y, W.
> T shakes hands with S, X, Y, W.

As can be seen from our chart, X, Y, W, Z, and T each have four hand-shakes. R and S each have one. So the minimum number of people needed to accomplish the required handshakes is seven. X, Y, W, Z, and T each have four handshakes, and R and S have one apiece for a total of twenty-two handshakes.

68. Below is a table showing different combinations and probabilities of the dice. From the total combinations, we can see that there are a total of thirty-six chances.

Total Number Showing on Dice	Total Combinations	Chances
2	1	1/36
3	2	2/36
4	3	3/36
5	4	4/36
6	5	5/36
7	6	6/36
8	5	5/36
9	4	4/36
10	3	3/36
11	2	2/36
12	1	1/36

You can see there are three ways to roll a 10 and six ways to roll a 7. Out of these nine possibilities, three are favorable for a win. Therefore, the chances for winning with 10 as a point are one in three.

69 Let's work this out.

Obviously, 10 must be in the top row, but it cannot be in either of the first two positions, since that would result in a duplication of 5's. Since 7 can only result from either 8 – 1 or 9 – 2, 8 and 9 must be in the top or next row. Nine can only result from 10 – 1, or it has to be in the top row. Therefore, 8 and 9 are not in the same row, and neither are 1 and 2, but all four numbers are in the top two rows. Out of the seven positions in the top two rows, we have 10, 9, 8, 1, 2, and 5 with 7 in the third row. That leaves 6, 3, or 4 for the remaining position in the top row. The digit next to the 7 can't be a 6 because that would result in duplicate 1's, and 6 cannot be the result of 7 minus any other number. Therefore, 6 is the remaining number of the seven numbers in the top two rows.

Six cannot be next to 5 or above 7, so it must be in the top row with 10. But 6 cannot be next to 10, so it is in the first or second position of the top row. And the number next to it must be 1. That means 9 cannot be in the top row; it would have to be next to 10, which would result in double 1's when subtracted. Eight must then be the other number in the top row.

That means the top row is 6 1 10 8, from which the remaining numbers can be generated:

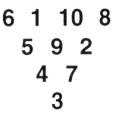

$$6 \quad 1 \quad 10 \quad 8$$
$$5 \quad 9 \quad 2$$
$$4 \quad 7$$
$$3$$

For numbers 1 through 15:

$$13 \quad 3 \quad 15 \quad 14 \quad 6$$
$$10 \quad 12 \quad 1 \quad 8$$
$$2 \quad 11 \quad 7$$
$$9 \quad 4$$
$$5$$

70. The two winning first moves are these.

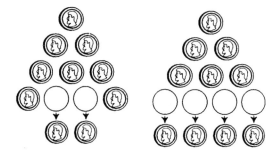

71. Here's one way the letter cross could look.

4265

8

3

1790

The total of the numbers used is 51 (17 × 3). The total of the numbers 1 through 9 is 45. There is a difference of 6. That difference is found in the letters D and G, since they are the only two letters counted twice. D and G must equal 6, and E + F must equal 11 to total 17 in the column. Since A = 4, D and G must be 1 and 5. The number 7 cannot be E or F. It would require the 4 to total 11. Also, 7 cannot be B, C, or D, since 4 + 7 would require the remaining two numbers in the top row to total 6, which is impossible. Therefore, 7 is in the bottom row with 0. That means the bottom row needs two numbers (besides 7 and 0) to total 10 for G + H + I + J to equal 17. One of those numbers must be 1 or 5. It can't be 5. You'd then have two 5's to total 10. Therefore, D = 5, G = 1, and the remaining number in the bottom row is 9. At this point the puzzle looks like this.

4BC5

E

F

1790

E + F must equal 11. The possible combinations are as follows.

$$2 + 9$$
$$3 + 8$$
$$4 + 7$$
$$5 + 6$$

The only possibility out of this group is 3 + 8, solving the values for D, E, F, and G, leaving 6 and 2 for B and C.

72. The next one is 46656.

Disregarding the number 1, these are the four consecutive lowest numbers that are both cubes and squares.

64	**729**	**4,096**
8^2 or 4^3	27^2 or 9^3	64^2 or 16^3

15,625	and the fifth,	**46,656**
125^2 or 25^3		216^2 or 36^3

73. Here's how to find the answer.

Since we know that Box C isn't the smallest, out of Boxes A, B, C, and D, Box D is the smallest. Its number is either 4 or 5.

The possible numbers for Box C are 2, 3, or 4 (not the largest or the smallest).

Box A can only be 2 or 3, since it is bigger than Box C or Box D, but it is not the biggest.

The total of Box C plus Box D must be at least 6 but not more than 7. The greatest possible sum of two different numbers between 1 and 5 is 7, assuming that sum is the equal to the sum of two other different numbers.

Since Box A is 2 or 3, and its number plus Box E's number must be at least 6, Box E is either 4 or 5.

Box A = 2 or 3
Box C = 2 or 3
Box D = 4 or 5
Box E = 4 or 5

We know that Box A is bigger than Box C, so Box A = 2, Box C = 3, Box D = 4, Box E = 5, and Box B = 1.

74. Three out of eight chances. Here are the possibilities.

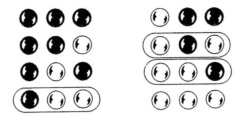

So, there are only three chances out of the eight possible combinations you could make.

75. Believe it or not, fifteen pieces (maximum) will result with four straight cuts through a cube.

This formula will give you the answer for any number of cuts. N = the number of cuts. So, three planar cuts yield eight pieces, four planar cuts yield fifteen pieces, five planar cuts yield twenty-six pieces, and six planar cuts yield forty-two pieces, and so on.

$$\left(\frac{N^3 + 5N}{6} \right) + 1 = \text{Number of Pieces}$$

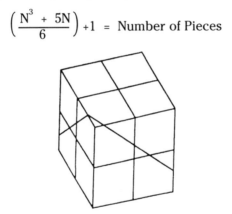

76. Let's see how its done. You only need to move five coins to turn the triangle upside down.

1—Move 3 to Row 3, outside 4.

2—Move 2 to Row 3, outside 6.

3—Move 1 to Row 6, between 12 and 13.

4—Move 15 to Row 6, between 13 and 14.

5—Move 11 to be the lone coin on the point of the upside-down triangle.

In general, where N is equal to the length of any side of a triangle (length in number of coins), the minimum number of coins that need

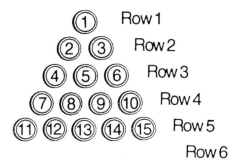

① Row 1
② ③ Row 2
④ ⑤ ⑥ Row 3
⑦ ⑧ ⑨ ⑩ Row 4
⑪ ⑫ ⑬ ⑭ ⑮ Row 5
Row 6

to be moved to turn that triangle upside down can be found by this formula.

$$\frac{N\,(N+1)}{6}$$

If the result of the division has a remainder, the answer is simply rounded down to the nearest whole number found in the quotient.

For example, if N = 7, then $\dfrac{7 \times 8}{6} = 6\,\overline{\smash{\big)}\,56} = 9$.

Rounding down to 9 will give the minimum number of coins needed to be moved in a triangle that has seven coins on a side.

Special thanks to mathematician Frank Bernhart (Rochester, N.Y.) for his assistance.

77. Here are the remaining moves.

7—Move 1 to 4.
8—Move 15 to 6.
9—Move 6 to 13.
10—Move 12 to 14.
11—Move 4 to 13.
12—Move 14 to 12.
13—Move 11 to 13.

78. Regardless of which face of Cube 1 you start with, the tunnel cannot exit through Cubes 3, 5, or 8.

79. This object requires six cubes to build. Here is its orthographic projection and the sixth side

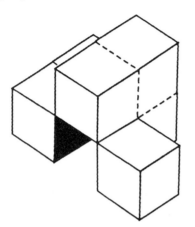 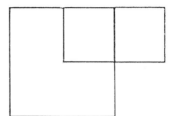

80. A man among men

81. Here's one way.

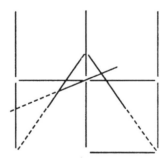

82. Far be it from me

83. If you are not careful, this short logic puzzle can be very confusing. Often, a solver's first instinct is to compare the speed and strength of each of the friends to determine their nicknames. Further inspection reveals that there isn't enough information to solve the puzzle that way. Here's where a grid of possibilities comes in handy.

We'll use X's and O's to fill in the grids. O will represent an elimination, and X will be a definite selection.

From a, we know that Pat can't be either Rabbit or Fly. So he must be either Bear or Walleye. We know from b that Tom cannot be either Rabbit or Walleye. So he must be either Bear or Fly. So, let's begin to fill in the chart.

	Rabbit	Fly	Walleye	Bear
Bob				
Bill				
Pat	O	O		
Tom	O		O	

From c, we know that Bob can't be Bear or Rabbit. Since he is faster than both Pat and Bear, Pat must be Walleye (since Pat was either Walleye or Bear).

As you can see from the final chart, Bill must be Rabbit, Tom has to be Bear, and Bob must be Fly.

	Rabbit	Fly	Walleye	Bear
Bob	O	X	O	O
Bill	X	O	O	O
Pat	O	O	X	O
Tom	O	O	O	X

84. We know that Brand A and Brand B equal 40 pounds. We also know that 40 pounds times $7 a pound will equal $280. We can set up two equations that can be solved simultaneously.

$$A + B = 40 \text{ pounds}$$
$$9A + 4B = \$280$$

Multiply the first equation by –9 to cancel out the A's.

$$-9A - 9B = -360$$
$$\underline{9A + 4B = 280}$$
$$-5B = -80$$

B = 16 and, therefore, A = 24 pounds.

85. Here's how you figure it out.

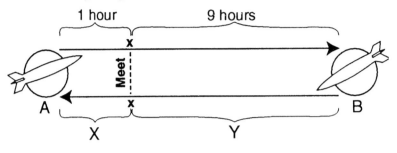

X + Y = total distance

V_f = velocity of faster rocket

V_s = velocity of slower rocket

T_b = time before meeting

Y = velocity of the faster rocket multiplied by the time before they meet ($V_f \times T_b$)

X = velocity of the slower rocket multiplied by the time before they meet ($V_s \times T_b$)

Therefore, $\dfrac{X}{Y} = \dfrac{V_s}{V_f}$

Now after the rockets meet, Y is equal to the slower velocity multiplied by 9, and X is equal to the faster velocity multiplied by one.

Thus: $\dfrac{X}{Y} = \dfrac{V_f}{9V_s}$

We now have two different fractions that represent $\dfrac{X}{Y}$, and they are equal.

$$\frac{V_s}{V_f} = \frac{V_f}{9V_s}$$

$$V_f^2 = 9V_s^2$$

$$\sqrt{V_f^2} = \sqrt{9V_s^2}$$

$$V_f = 3V_s$$

The faster rocket is going three times as fast as the slower rocket.

86. Let's call the first system X and the second system Y.

X	Y
14	36
133	87

In order to get an idea of some relationship between the two systems, we'll subtract 14 from 133 (119) and compare that to the difference of 87 minus 36 (51). We can compare 119 to 51, but first, let's reduce it by dividing by 17, giving us 7 to 3. For every seven degrees on the X thermometer, Y will grow or decrease by three. When X is at 14°, if we move toward X becoming 0°, Y will be reduced by 6°. When X is 0°, Y = 30°, giving us the formula Y = $^3/_7$X + 30.

To find the temperature at which both thermometers read the same, set Y to equal X, and the formula then becomes:

$$X = {}^3/_7X + 30$$
$$^4/_7X = 30$$
$$4X = 210$$
$$X = 52.5°$$

87. There are three different shapes to consider: a square, a loop, and two connecting lines. Figures A, B, and C each use two of the shapes. These first three figures form a pattern. Beginning with Figure D, the sequence continues. To get Figure D, Figure A was rotated 90° to the right. Figure E is really Figure B rotated 90° to the right. Therefore, the sixth figure will be Figure C rotated 90° to the right.

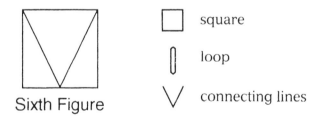

Sixth Figure

☐ square

loop

V connecting lines

88. The answer is D. The other four figures have both concave and convex components. Figure D has convex parts only.

89. The only thing you have to go on are the names of the people and the letters in their names. After a little inspection, you'll find each letter of the name is equivalent to three of "them," whatever "them" may be. Mary Les has seven letters in her name, therefore she has twenty-one of "them."

90. There are twenty-five individual cubes.

91. This is a good example of a problem or puzzle that can be broken into smaller components to determine a pattern.

If one person walks into a theater to take one seat, that person has only one choice. If two people occupy two seats, this can happen in two different ways. Three people occupying three seats (following the condition that each subsequent person sits next to another) can be accomplished in four different ways. Four people in four seats produce eight ways. We'll make a table to see what we have.

Number of People	Possible Combinations
1	1
2	2
3	4
4	8
5	?

As can be seen, with each additional person and seat, the different orders increase by a power of two. For five people in five seats, there are sixteen different possible combinations. For any number N, it can be seen that $2^{(N-1)}$ will give the correct answer. So, for twelve people, 4096 different combinations are possible:

$$2^{(13-1)} = 2^{12} = 4096.$$

92 There were 20 nickels and 20 dimes. To solve this, set up the following equations, where n = nickels and d = dimes:

$$n = d$$
$$.05n + .10d = 3.00$$
$$.05n + .10n = 3.00$$
$$.15n = 3.00$$
$$n = 20$$

93. x = 5, y = 6, and z = 4, so the sum is 15. The variable x can be either 0 or 5. It must be 5 because there is no number that ends in 0 when multiplied by 7 ($y \times 7$, resulting in x). Therefore, a 3 is carried over to the y. Since x is 5, y must be 6 because 7 × 6 = 42. Add the 3 that was carried over and you get 45. Therefore, z is 4.

94. It might be helpful to set up a grid as follows:

	Basketball	Football	Baseball
Alex	x		o
Ryan	o		
Steven	x	o	x

We can see that Ryan must like basketball since neither Alex nor Steven does. Steven does not like basketball or baseball, so he must like football, leaving Alex liking baseball.

95. Seven zips have the weight of 1 wob. The problem can be set up as follows:

$$26z = 4c + 2w$$
$$8z + 2c = 2w$$

Rearranging, we get

$$(1)\ 26z = 4c + 2w$$
$$(2)\ 8z = -2c + 2w$$

Multiply equation (2) by 2 so that the c factor drops out, and combine the two equations:

$$
\begin{array}{rl}
26z = & 4c + 2w \\
\underline{16z = } & \underline{-4c + 4w} \\
42z = & 6w \\
7z = & w
\end{array}
$$

96. Look before you leap.

97. The missing number is 10. The numbers in each circle add up to 50.

98 The answer is 96. Set up the following equations:

$$\tfrac{1}{2} \times \tfrac{2}{3} \times \tfrac{3}{5} = \tfrac{6}{30} = \tfrac{1}{5}$$
$$\tfrac{1}{5} \times 240 = 48$$
$$48 \div \tfrac{1}{2} = 96$$

99. It's the right thing to do.

100. The answer is "three words."

101. The next letter is P. The letters missing between letters in the series form the pattern 1, 2, 1, 2, 1, 2...

102. Figure 4 is the only one that doesn't contain a triangle.

103. The lesser of two evils.

104. It is impossible to average 60 miles per hour for this trip. At 30 miles per hour, the car would travel one mile in two minutes; at 60 miles per hour, the car would travel two miles in two minutes. So, in order to average 60 mph, the entire trip of two miles would have to be completed in two minutes. But the driver has already used two minutes going from point A to point B; there's not time left to get from point B to point C.

105. Here's one way to solve the puzzle:

TOOK
BOOK
BOON
BORN
BURN

106. 6.25 percent. Remember, length $\times$ width = area. Let l = length and w = width. Then

$$l + .25l = 1.25l$$
$$w - .25w = .75w$$
$$1.25l \times .75w = 93.75$$

Finally,

$$100 - 93.75 = 6.25$$

107. The chances are 1 in 3. Here are all the possible draws (C1 = first cherry gumdrop, C2 = second cherry gumdrop, O = orange gumdrop):

First draw	Second draw
C1	C2
C1	O
C2	C1
C2	O
O	C1
O	C2

Among the six possible draws, O appears twice in the second draw column; thus the chances are 2 in 6, or 1 in 3.

108. Five.

109. The "R" goes above the line. The letters above the line are closed with a space inside them.

110. Time slips into the future.

111. There are 100 years in a century.

112. Let x = the fraction. Then:

$$(3 \times \tfrac{1}{4}x) \times x = \tfrac{1}{12}$$
$$\tfrac{3}{4}x^2 = \tfrac{1}{12}$$
$$x^2 = \tfrac{1}{9}$$
$$x = \tfrac{1}{3}$$

113. Two miles. They are actually eating up the distance at 120 miles per hour (50 + 70):

$$\frac{120 \text{ miles}}{60 \text{ minutes}} = \text{two miles in one minute}$$

114. Pocket full of money.

115. They can be combined in 12 different ways.

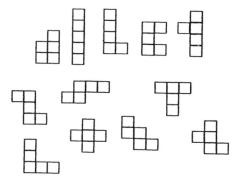

116. 1/24

$$\frac{3}{32} - \frac{1}{16} = \frac{1}{32}$$

$$4 \times \left(\frac{1}{3} \times \frac{1}{32}\right) = \frac{4}{96} \text{ or } \frac{1}{24}$$

117. The letters "mot" will create the words "mother," "motion," "motor," "motif," and "motto."

118. The answer is (e). Remember, x may be a negative number.

119. He would have 20 pleezorns. Count the letters in each name and multiply by 2.

120. $.1 \times .9 \times .8 = .072 = 7.2\%$

121. Line dance

122. The ratio is 1 to 2. One way to solve this problem is to set up an equation in which x equals the amount of $48 chemical used and y equals the amount of $36 chemical used:

$$48x + 36y = 40(x + y)$$
$$48x + 36y = 40x + 40y$$
$$8x = 4y$$
$$\frac{x}{y} = \frac{1}{2}$$

123. Traffic jam

124. There are 31 triangles.

125. The ratio is 1 to 2. It might help to set up the problem as follows:

$$\frac{5x}{4y} = \frac{7}{8}$$
$$40x = 28y$$
$$10x = 7y$$

Thus, $10x$ to $7y$ is a 1-to-1 relationship. We are asked for the ratio of $10x$ to $14y$; since $14 = 7 \times 2$, we can see that it is a 1-to-2 relationship.

126. Don't count your chickens before they hatch.

127. Three-ring circus

128. Here are 21 four-letter words:

twin	wine	lint
kiln	kilt	lent
wink	wilt	like
link	welt	kine
tine	tile	lien
newt	kite	line
went	wile	knit

129. The answer is 13,222.

$$12,000$$
$$+1,222$$
$$13,222$$

130. JJ. The letters are the initial letters of pairs of month names, starting with October-November.

131. Forward thinking

132. Double-decker sandwich

133. Draw a line as follows and you'll see the answer, June:

134. $4^6 + 6^4$ . . . by more than double

135. Microorganism

136. There is one wheel on a unicycle.

137. Fifteen angles of less than 90 degrees can be formed.

138. Here they are:

$$\frac{1}{2} = \frac{6,729}{13,458}$$

$$\frac{1}{3} = \frac{5,832}{17,496}$$

$$\frac{1}{4} = \frac{4,392}{17,568}$$

$$\frac{1}{5} = \frac{2,769}{13,845}$$

$$\frac{1}{6} = \frac{2,943}{17,658}$$

$$\frac{1}{7} = \frac{2,394}{16,758}$$

$$\frac{1}{8} = \frac{3,187}{25,496}$$

$$\frac{1}{9} = \frac{6,381}{57,429}$$

139. i before e except after c

140. The missing numbers are 18 and 5, respectively. There are actually two separate series of numbers in this puzzle. Look at every other number, beginning first with 8 and then with 15.

141. The value of **z** must be 9 in all cases.

142. The value of **x** is 1. The variable **y** can have any of a number of values, but **x** must always equal 1 and **z** must always equal 9.

143. Yes. A number is divisible by 8 if its last three digits are divisible by 8. Examples: 6,240; 9,184; 15,536.

144. Doorbell. All the rest have handles.

145. You would write it 17 times. Don't forget that there are two 4s in 44!

146. Figure C is the only figure without a straight line.

147. Right cross followed by an uppercut.

148. For these three numbers, 455 is the lowest common denominator.

149. Fill in the blanks.

150. 107 percent of 300 is greater. Because 107 percent is equivalent to 1.07, we have

$$1.07 \times 300 = 321$$
$$.50 \times 600 = 300$$

151. The answer is $^{10}/_{33}$. The problem can be solved as follows:

$$\cfrac{1}{3+\cfrac{1}{3\frac{1}{3}}} = \cfrac{1}{3+\cfrac{1}{\frac{10}{3}}} = \cfrac{1}{3+\cfrac{3}{10}} = \cfrac{1}{\frac{33}{10}} = \frac{10}{33}$$

152.

1	8	13	12
14	11	2	7
4	5	16	9
15	10	3	6

153. Here's one way:

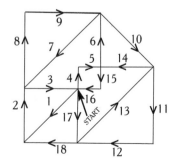

154. You would receive 221 silver pieces. If you were to exchange your kooklas only for gold, it would require 40 × 7 or 280 pieces. But there are only 161 gold pieces, leaving you 119 gold pieces short. The value of silver coins to gold coins is in the ratio of 13 to 7:

$$\frac{13}{7} = \frac{x}{119}$$
$$7x = 1{,}547$$
$$x = 221$$

155. The missing number is 35. The second number in each box is the square of the first number minus 1.

156. There are 720 possible arrangements. Use the following equation to solve the problem (this is called factorial notation):

$$6! = 6 \times 5 \times 4 \times 3 \times 2 \times 1 = 720$$

157. Hole in one

158. The number 9 goes below the line and the number 10 goes above it—the numbers 1, 2, 6, and 10 are all spelled with three letters; the rest have four or more.

159. Your eyes are bigger than your stomach.

160. Here are two examples:
1. When giving yes and no answers, a person who tells a lie about a lie is telling the truth.
2. Imagine a child rolling his wagon backward down a hill. If you were to film this and run the film backward, you would see the wagon going forward up the hill.

161. Algebra

162. $8\frac{88}{88}$

163. There are 24 cubes.

164. They say at least 100 words can be made from "Thanksgiving." How many can you find?

165. It is $^7/_9$. The problem can be approached as follows:

$$^1/_{10} \div \, ^1/_2 \div \, ^1/_5 = \, ^1/_{10} \times 2 \times 5 = 1$$
$$1 \times \, ^7/_9 = \, ^7/_9$$

166. Elbow grease

167. x, y, and z = 8, 12, and 60 pounds, respectively. Starting with the 8 ft. section:

$$8 \text{ ft.} \times 10 \text{ lbs.} = 80 \text{ ft.-lbs.}$$

To balance, the bottom left part of the mobile must also equal 80 ft.-lbs., so its total weight must be 20 lbs. (4 ft. × 20 lbs. = 80 ft.-lbs.) Therefore,

$$x + y = 20$$
and
$$6x = 4y.$$
So, $y = 20 - x$
and substituting,
$$6x = 4(20 - x)$$
$$6x = 80 - 4x$$
$$10x = 80$$
$$x = 8$$
and therefore,
$$y = 12.$$

Adding the total weights of the left side, we have
$$120 + 10 + 8 + 12 = 150 \text{ lbs.}$$
$$150 \text{ lbs.} \times 4 \text{ ft.} = 600 \text{ ft.-lbs.}$$

Therefore, the right side must also be 600 ft.-lbs.:
$$10 \text{ ft.} \times z \text{ lbs.} = 600 \text{ ft.-lbs.}$$
$$z = 60$$

168. All answers are divisible by nine.

169. The square is 6 feet by 6 feet. To solve this problem, let x represent each side of the square. Then

$$4x = x^2 \times \frac{2}{3}$$
$$12x = 2x^2$$
$$6x = x^2$$
$$x = 6$$

170. Shrinking violets

171. 2 in 9. Because each die has 6 faces, there are 6 × 6 or 36 possible combinations of numbers. Of these, 6 combinations result in a 7:

6 and 1

1 and 6

5 and 2

2 and 5

4 and 3

3 and 4

And 2 combinations result in an 11:

5 and 6

6 and 5

thus the chances are 8 in 36, or 2 in 9.

172. Calm before the storm

173.

MOOD

MOON

MORN

BORN

BARN

174. T = 15. Since A = 2, we can substitute A into the first four equations to come up with the following:

(1) $2 + B = H$

(2) $H + P = T$

(3) $T + 2 = F$

(4) $B + P + F = 30$

Now substitute equation (1) into equation (2):

$(2 + B) + P = T$

Rearranging, we get

$B + P = T - 2$

Substitute this into equation (4):

$(T - 2) + F = 30$

Finally, substitute equation (3) into equation (4) and solve for T:

$(T - 2) + (T + 2) = 30$

$2T = 30$

$T = 15$

175. An onion costs 7 cents. Set up the equations, with x as potatoes and y as onions:

$$5x + 6y = 1.22$$
$$6x + 5y = 1.31$$

Multiply the first equation by 6, the second one by 5:

$$30x + 36y = 7.32$$
$$30x + 25y = 6.55$$

Subtract the second equation from the first, and you have:

$$0x + 11y = .77$$
$$y = .07$$

176. Rising tide

177. It can be done as follows:

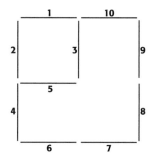

178. $A: \dfrac{343}{1000}$ $B: \dfrac{7}{24}$

On any given single draw with all 10 balls in the box, there is a 7 in 10 chance of drawing a green ball. So the probability of all 3 balls chosen being green is:

$$\frac{7}{10} \times \frac{7}{10} \times \frac{7}{10} = \frac{343}{1000} = 34.3\%$$

If the balls are not replaced in the bag:

The chance on the first draw is 7 in 10; on the second draw, it is 6 in 9; and on the third draw, it is 5 in 8. So the probability of 3 balls being in pulled in succession if they are not replaced is:

$$\frac{7}{10} \times \frac{6}{9} \times \frac{5}{8} = \frac{210}{720} \text{ or } \frac{7}{24} = 29.2\%$$

179. The missing number is zero. If you convert each fraction to twelfths, you get the following series:

$$\frac{5}{12} \qquad \frac{4}{12} \qquad \frac{3}{12} \qquad \frac{2}{12} \qquad \frac{1}{12} \qquad 0$$

180. Multiplication tables

181. There are 206 bones in the human body.

182. Factors of the number 12 (6 + 4 + 3 + 2 + 1) add up to 16.

183. 18. $\frac{1}{4}$ of $\frac{1}{3}$ of $\frac{1}{6}$ is $\frac{1}{72}$; $\frac{1}{72}$ of 432 is 6; and 6 divided by $\frac{1}{3}$ is 18.

184. Deep in thought

185. Fifty-six applicants have experience in selling both golf equipment and athletic shoes. Since 13 of the applicants have had no sales experience, we're dealing with 87 people who have some experience. Of the 87 applicants, 65 of them have sold golf equipment, which means that 22 of this group haven't sold golf equipment (87 – 65 = 22). Seventy-eight of the applicants have sold shoes, which means that 9 haven't (87 – 78 = 9). Therefore, we have 9 + 22 or 31 people who could not have sold both—thus, 87 – 31 = 56 people who *have* had experience in selling both.

186. 110 square yards. An area 11 yards square measures 11 yards on each of four sides and therefore has a total of 121 square yards. An area of 11 square yards, if it were square, would be just under 3.32 yards on each side. The difference between the two, then, is found by subtracting 11 square yards from 121 square yards: 110 square yards.

187. Life

188. You are on time.

189. 6009, 6119

190. Seven. These are the elements hydrogen, carbon, and nitrogen with their respective atomic numbers; seven is the atomic number for nitrogen.

191. Can't see the forest for the trees

192. They are 496 and 8,128. The next perfect number after that is 33,550,336!

193. There are 16 possibilities, each having a probability of $^1/_{16}$. There are 6 ways with exactly 2 tails, 4 ways with 3 tails, and 1 way with 4 tails. That's a total of 11 ways out of 16. The chances are 11 in 16.

HHHH	TTTT
HTTT	THHH
HHHT	TTTH
HTHH	THTT
HHTH	TTHT
HHTT	TTHH
HTHT	THTH
HTTH	THHT

194. A break in the action

195. Let a smile be your umbrella.

196. 27,000. The repeating pattern is, respectively, 2, 3, and 5 times the preceding number.

197.

198. It will take 1.2 hours.
The equation can be set up this way:

$$\frac{x}{3} + \frac{x}{2} = 1$$

Multiply by 6:

$$2x + 3x = 6$$
$$5x = 6$$
$$x = \frac{6}{5} = 1.2$$

199. I am 19 years old and my sister is 9.
Let x = my sister's age and y = my age.
$$y = x + 10 \text{ and}$$
$$y + 1 = 2(x + 1)$$
$$y = 2x + 1$$
Substituting this result in our first equation, we have
$$2x + 1 = x + 10$$
$$x = 9$$
so
$$y = 19.$$
When my sister was 5, I was 3 times older than she was.

200. The missing letter is S. These are the first letters of the even numbers when spelled out, beginning with two.

201. Upside-down cake

202. Sally Billingsley and Susie Jenkins are the real names. Because one of the first two statements had to be false, the third statement also had to be false.

203. The square of 95 is 9,025. There are several ways this can be done. Here's one way. It helps to remember that any number ending in 5, when squared, will always end in 25.

Go to the number ending in 0 directly above the number ending in 5—in this case 100. Now go to the number ending in 0 directly below the number ending in 5—in this case 90.

In your mind square 100 (10,000) and square 90 (8,100). Add these two numbers together (18,100) and divide by 2 (9,050); then replace the last two digits with 25. So the square of 95 is 9,025.

Now, come up with another way to do this.

204. The missing letter is N; the word is "sandwich."

205. Power surge

206. None. Instead, turn the puzzle upside-down and add:

$$
\begin{array}{r}
86 \\
91 \\
+68 \\
\hline
245
\end{array}
$$

207. 20 percent. Say there are 10 caramels. Since the number of caramels is 25 percent of the number of other candies, there must be 40 pieces of candy that aren't caramels. The total number of pieces of candy = 10 + 40 = 50, so $^{10}/_{50} = ^1/_5 = 20$ percent.

208. Fender bender

209. There are 106 elements in the periodic table.

210. Here's one way to solve the puzzle:

$$\begin{array}{c} \text{ROAD} \\ \text{ROAM} \\ \text{ROOM} \\ \text{LOOM} \\ \text{LOOP} \end{array}$$

211. Diagram E is the odd one out. The other four are symmetrical about both of their axes: if you turn them 90 degrees, they will look the same as in their original positions.

212.

C	=	100
D	=	500
$\overline{M}$	=	1,000
$\overline{V}$	=	5,000
$\overline{X}$	=	10,000
$\overline{L}$	=	50,000
$\overline{C}$	=	100,000
$\overline{D}$	=	500,000
$\overline{M}$	=	1,000,000

213. Current affair

214. Here are some 10-letter words.

Typewriter	Proprietor	Tetterwort
Pepperroot	Pirouetter	Repertoire
Pepperwort	Prerequire	Perpetuity

215. Central Intelligence Agency

216. The chances are still 1 in 50.

217. The missing number is $1/30$. The series is constructed as follows:

$$12 = \tfrac{1}{7} \text{ of } 84$$

$$2 = \tfrac{1}{6} \text{ of } 12$$

$$\tfrac{2}{5} = \tfrac{1}{5} \text{ of } 2$$

$$\tfrac{1}{10} = \tfrac{1}{4} \text{ of } \tfrac{2}{5}$$

$$\tfrac{1}{30} = \tfrac{1}{3} \text{ of } \tfrac{1}{10}$$

218. Guilty beyond a reasonable doubt

219. $96. Use the equation

$$\tfrac{1}{4}x - (\tfrac{3}{4} \times \tfrac{1}{4}x) = \$6$$

$$\tfrac{1}{4}x - \tfrac{3}{16}x = \$6$$

Multiply each side by 16:

$$4x - 3x = \$96$$

$$x = \$96$$

220. She is their aunt.

221. "Lapy" means tree. From the first two phrases, "rota" must mean apple. From the third phrase, "mena" must mean large, leaving "lapy" to be tree.

222. Hologram

223. The numbers in each circle add up to 150, so the missing number is 23.

224. The missing number is 7. The numbers have a one-to-one correspondence with the letters of the alphabet, where A = 1, B = 2, C = 3, and so forth. The word spelled out is "mind-bending."

225. No time left on the clock

226. Book

227. There are 180 degrees in a triangle.

228. The chance of drawing the ace of spades is 1 in 52; for the king, 1 in 51; for the queen, 1 in 50; and for the jack, 1 in 49. To calculate the answer, multiply these altogether:

$$\frac{1}{52} \times \frac{1}{51} \times \frac{1}{50} \times \frac{1}{49} = \frac{1}{6,497,400}$$

229.

$$\frac{34}{650} \text{ or } \frac{17}{325}$$

$\frac{1}{10}$ less than $\frac{3}{13}$ is:

$$\frac{30}{130} - \frac{13}{130} = \frac{17}{130}$$

4 times $\frac{1}{10}$ of that number is:

$$4 \times \frac{1}{10} \times \frac{17}{130} = \frac{4}{10} \times \frac{17}{130}$$
$$= \frac{2}{5} \times \frac{17}{130}$$
$$= \frac{34}{650}$$
$$= \frac{17}{325}$$

230.

$$\begin{array}{r} 70,839 \\ - 6,458 \\ \hline 64,381 \end{array}$$

The answer to the "SEND + MORE = MONEY" puzzle is:

$$\begin{array}{r} 9,567 \\ + 1,085 \\ \hline 10,652 \end{array}$$

231. There are 19 squares.

232. Slim chance

233. Knock on wood.

234.

BIKE
BITE
MITE
MATE
MATH

235. POTS, SPOT, and OPTS. These are the only three remaining four-letter words that can be made by using the letters O, P, S, and T only once.

236. The missing number is 6. Keep taking the differences between numbers (keeping in mind positive and negative differences) and you get:

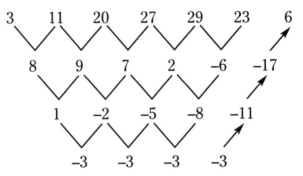

237. Transparent

238. Dirty dozen

239. With players for each match through six rounds, 2^6 or 64 players are entered.

240. There are 24 letters in the Greek alphabet.

241. Five. Square 1 is the largest square and frames the whole figure. Then square 2 is placed in the lower right corner, and square 3 is placed in the upper left corner. (Square 2 and square 3 are the same size.) Square 4 is placed over square 3 in the upper-left corner, and square 5 is placed in the middle.

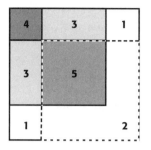

242. Each layer would contain a number of balls equal to the square of the layer. In other words, layer 1 (the top layer) would have $1^2 = 1$ ball; layer 2 would have $2^2 = 4$ balls; layer 3 would have $3^2 = 9$ balls; and so on. The layers would stack up like this, for a total of 140 balls.

$$
\begin{array}{r}
1 \\
4 \\
6 \\
25 \\
36 \\
\underline{49} \\
140
\end{array}
$$

243. Close shave

244. Starting with the bottom row, determine if two adjacent circles are different colors. A black circle goes above and between different-colored circles. A white circle goes above and between same-colored circles. The top of the pyramid is shown below.

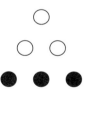

245. From left to right, the weights are 200 lbs., 120 lbs., 102 lbs., and 68 lbs.

First we find the two weights on the left. Their total weight (call it a) at a distance of 4 ft. must balance 160 lbs. at a distance of 8 ft.:

$$4a = 8 \times 160$$
$$a = 1{,}280 \div 4 = 320 \text{ lbs.}$$

Then $\frac{5}{8}$ of this weight at 3 ft. must balance $\frac{3}{8}$ of this weight at 5 ft.:

$$\frac{5}{8} \times 320 = 200 \text{ lbs. and } \frac{3}{8} \times 320 = 120 \text{ lbs.}$$

Next we find the two weights on the right. Their total weight (call it b) at a distance of 12 ft. must balance $200 + 120 + 160 + 30 = 510$ lbs. at a distance of 4 ft.:

$$12b = 4 \times 510$$
$$b = 2040 \div 12 = 170 \text{ lbs.}$$

Then $\frac{6}{10}$ of this weight at 4 ft. must balance $\frac{4}{10}$ of this weight at 6 ft.:

$$\frac{6}{10} \times 170 = 102 \text{ lbs. and } \frac{4}{10} \times 170 = 68 \text{ lbs.}$$

246. The proof is in the pudding.

247. Four people can sit in five seats as follows:
$5 \times 4 \times 3 \times 2$, for a total of 120 different ways.

248 Shine

249. The best approach to this problem is to find a common denominator of 2, 4, and 7 that is less than 30—that is 28. Then add up the calculated numbers of students:

2 students received a B

$\frac{1}{4}$ of 28 = 7 students failed

$\frac{1}{2}$ of 28 = 14 students received a D

$\frac{1}{7}$ of 28 = 4 students received a C

totalling 27, which means only 1 student received an A.

250. 1 day. Let x be the number of days it would take all three to build the fence. In 1 day the total of their individual contributions to building the fence would be:

$$\frac{x}{2} + \frac{x}{3} + \frac{x}{6} = 1$$

$$\frac{3x}{6} + \frac{2x}{6} + \frac{x}{6} = \frac{6}{6}$$

$$6x = 6$$

$$x = 1 \text{ day}$$

251. Foreign correspondent

252. 441. Use the following formula to find the number of cubes when the width, length, and height of the stack have the same number of cubes.

Let c = that number of cubes.

$$c^3 + (c-1)^3 + (c-2)^3 + (c-3)^3 \ldots (c-c)^3$$
$$\text{So,}$$
$$6^3 + 5^3 + 4^3 + 3^3 + 2^3 + 1^3 =$$
$$216 + 125 + 64 + 27 + 8 + 1 = 441$$
$$\text{total cubes.}$$

253. Here's one way. Can you find others?

2	10

5	8	6

3	1	4

9	7

281

254. 4 to 1. Here is one way to solve this:

$$\text{if } p = \frac{3}{4}q, \text{ then } q = \frac{4}{3}p$$

$$\text{if } q = \frac{2}{3}r, \text{ then } r = \frac{3}{2}q \text{ and}$$

$$\text{if } r = \frac{1}{2}s, \text{ then } s = \frac{2}{1}r$$

Therefore,

$$s \text{ to } p \text{ is } \frac{2}{1} \times \frac{3}{2} \times \frac{4}{3} = \frac{24}{6} = 4 \text{ to } 1$$

255. Safety in numbers

256.   first base: Reggie
     catcher: Lou
     right field: Leo
     left field: Chris

Here's how to deduce the answer from the given facts:

Reggie: From the question we know that Reggie can't play right field. From point (a) we know that Reggie isn't the catcher or the left fielder, so he must be the first baseman.

Leo: From the question we know that Leo can't be the catcher, and from point (b) we know that Leo can't be the left fielder. He can't play first base because that's Reggie's position, so he must be the right fielder.

Lou: From the question we know that Lou can't play left field. He can't play first base (Reggie's position) or right field (Leo's position), so he must be the catcher.

Chris: With all the other positions filled, Chris must be the left fielder.

257. Golden anniversary

258. The letter e.

259.
     BAND
     BIND
     BINS
     PINS
     PIPS

260. 2 to 3. Let the bicycle's current age be $3x$ making the tires' age x when the bicycle was old as the tires are now. To make them the same age we must add to the tires' age some number, y, and subtract from the bicycle's age the same number, y:

$$\underline{\text{bike's age} \quad \text{tires' age}}$$
$$2x - y = x + y$$
$$2x = 2y$$
$$x = y$$

Since we've already established that $x = y$, we can substitute y for x in the bike's current age:

$$3x = 3y$$

The tires' current age is then $2y$, and the ratio of the tires' current age to the bicycle's current age is $2y/3y$, a ratio of 2 to 3.

261.

$$2^{13}, \text{ by a lot}$$
$$2^{13} = 8,192$$
$$\text{but}$$
$$2^{12} + 2^2 = 4,096 + 4 = 4,100$$

262. Four score and seven years ago

263. Repeating rifles

264.

$$
\begin{array}{r}
73544 \\
73544 \\
73544 \\
+494046 \\
\hline
714678
\end{array}
$$

265. Number the grids as shown below, designating the row and column of each box. The sum of the numbers in the marked boxes in the first grids (11 + 21 and 12 + 31) equal the numbers in the marked boxes in the second grids (32 and 43, respectively).

	12	13
	22	23
31		33

11		13	14
21	22	23	24
	32	33	34
41	42		44

266. Connect the dots

267. $9 \times 8 \times 7 \times 6 \times 5 \times 4 \times 3 \times 2 \times 1 = 362,880$ different seating arrangements. In mathematics, this is written "9!" and called "factorial 9."

268.

1. gambol	k. frolic
2. fortissimo	c. loud
3. sortie	l. raid
4. millinery	b. hats
5. culinary	i. cooking
6. ornithology	n. birds
7. odoriferous	f. smell
8. gustatory	o. taste
9. humus	m. soil
10. terrapin	a. turtle
11. bovine	j. cow
12. antipodes	h. opposites
13. equivocal	e. ambiguous
14. potentate	d. power
15. urbane	g. refined

269. There is sufficient information. The ladder is 25 feet long. A diagram helps in the solution:

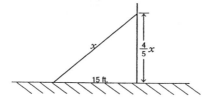

The ladder leaning against the wall makes a triangle. Let's call the ladder's length x. Since the top slid down to a point four-fifths of the ladder's length up the wall, we know that that side is $^4/_5x$. The base of the triangle is 15 feet, which is the distance the foot of the ladder slid along the ground. Using the Pythagorean theorem ($c^2 = a^2 + b^2$), we can find the length of the ladder:

$$x^2 = (\tfrac{4}{5}x)^2 + 225$$

$$x^2 = \frac{16}{25}x^2 + 225$$

$$25x^2 = 16x^2 + 5625$$

$$9x^2 = 5625$$

$$x^2 = 625$$

$$x = 25 \text{ ft.}$$

270. 70.

> $1f = 10k$
> $1c = 6f = 6 \times 10k = 60k$
> $1w = 5c = 5 \times 60k = 300k$
> $1n = 7w = 7 \times 300k = 2100k$

Thus, there are 2100 krits in a nood. We also see that

> $1w = 300k = 30(10k) = 30f$

Therefore, there are 30 fligs in a wirp.

271. Two wrongs don't make a right.

272. Out to lunch

273. MMX̌DXLIV

274. 162 and 1.

Starting at left, every other number is multiplied by 3. Starting at right, every other number is also multiplied by 3.

275. $4^4 + 44 = 300$

276. It would appear in column B. Divide by 7 whatever number you wish to place, and see what the remainder is. If the remainder is 1, the number goes in column A; if the remainder is 2, the number goes in column B; and so on. (If the remainder is zero, however, the number goes in column G.)

277. Audrey will reach the destination first. Suppose they cover 12 miles, both walking at a rate of 2 miles per hour and running at a rate of 6 miles per hour. Use the formula
$rt = d$ (rate $\times$ time = distance) to find each person's time.
Nancy (walks half the distance and runs half the distance):

$$2t = 6 \text{ mi., so } t = 3 \text{ hrs. walking}$$
$$6t = 6 \text{ mi., so } t = 1 \text{ hr. running}$$
$$t = 4 \text{ hours total time}$$

Audrey (walks half the time and runs half the time):

$$2(\tfrac{1}{2}t) + 6(\tfrac{1}{2}t) = 12 \text{ mi.}$$
$$t + 3t = 12$$
$$4t = 12$$
$$t = 3 \text{ hours total time}$$

278. Each reads the same when held upside down.

279. Lead by example.

280. Simply add the sum of the two digits in any number to the sum of the two digits in the adjacent number to get the corresponding number in the row below. For example:

$$8 + 9 \ (89) \text{ and } 5 + 3 \ (53) = 25$$
$$5 + 3 \ (53) \text{ and } 1 + 7 \ (17) = 16$$

To find the missing number, add:

$$1 + 6 \ (16) \text{ and } 1 + 7 \ (17) = 15$$

281. His younger daughter received more—$4,000 more—than the older daughter. One way to solve this is to set up an equation that represents who received what:

$$x = \frac{1}{3}x + \frac{1}{5}x + \frac{1}{6}x + 9{,}000$$

$$x = \frac{10}{30}x + \frac{6}{30}x + \frac{5}{30}x + 9{,}000$$

$$x = \frac{21}{30}x + 9{,}000$$

Multiplying both sides of the equation by $\frac{30}{9}$, we get

$$\frac{30}{9}x = \frac{21}{9}x + \frac{270{,}000}{9}$$

$$\frac{30}{9}x - \frac{21}{9}x = 30{,}000$$

$$x = 30{,}000$$

Then

$$\frac{1}{3}x = \$10{,}000 \text{ (wife)}$$

$$\frac{1}{5}x = \$6{,}000 \text{ (son)}$$

$$\frac{1}{6}x = \$5{,}000 \text{ (older daughter)}$$

282. The missing number is 4. Simply add the first and second rows together to get the third row, like this:

$$\begin{array}{r} 65{,}927 \\ \underline{14{,}354} \\ 80{,}281 \end{array}$$

283. In 60 days. If one clock gains a minute a day (or loses, the math will be the same), it will gain 24 minutes the first day, 48 minutes by the end of the second, and 120 minutes after 5 days. This means in ten days it will gain 4 hours and in 20 days, 8 hours. This times 3, to make it 24 hours, will require 60 days. The other clock running backward will tell the same time as the normal clock every 24 hours, so it really doesn't present a problem for the solution of the puzzle.

284. Cheaper by the dozen

285. Pages 6, 19, and 20 are also missing. Newspapers are printed double sided, two pages to a sheet. The first and second pages are attached to the second-to-last and last pages—in this case, pages 23 and 24. The rest of the pages are attached as follows:

1–2 with 23–24
3–4 with 21–22
5–6 with 19–20
7–8 with 17–18
9–10 with 15–16
11–12 with 13–14

286. The value of c is 14. To solve the problem, set up the following equations:

$$(1)\ a + b = 13$$
$$(2)\ b + c = 22$$
$$(3)\ a + c = 19$$

Solve for b in equation (1):

$$b = 13 - a$$

Substitute this into equation (2):

$$13 - a + c = 22$$
$$-a + c = 9$$

Then combine equations (2) and (3) and solve for c:

$$-a + c = 9$$
$$\underline{a + c = 19}$$
$$2c = 28$$
$$c = 14$$

287. Rotate the first square 90 degrees to the right to obtain the second square.

	X	
X		
		X

288.

MOVE
MORE
MARE
BARE
BARK

289. Sarah is the second oldest; Liz is the oldest.

290. The missing number is 14. The first and last numbers added together make 19, as do the second number and the next-to-last number. Moving toward the middle in this fashion, each successive pair of numbers adds up to 19.

291. Broken promise

292. There are 23 triangles.

293. $(4! \times 4 + 4)/4$ is one answer. Did you find another?

294. You are out of touch.

295. e. $\dfrac{1}{10\sqrt{10}}$

296. Carrot juice (The symbol before "juice" is called a "caret.")

297. The chances are 1 in 5. The possibilities are:

$Blue_1$, $Blue_2$
$Blue_1$, Green
$Blue_1$, Yellow
$Blue_2$, Green
$Blue_2$, Yellow

298. Yardstick

299. $16^2/_3$ lbs. Calculate the answer as follows:

1) A + B = 50 lbs.
and 2) \$8A + \$5B = 50 × \$6

Then, multiply the first equation by –5, so:

–5A – 5B = –250

Next, combine with equation 2:

$$\$8A + \$5B = \$300$$
$$\underline{-5A - \ 5B = -250}$$
$$3A = \ \ \ 50$$
$$A = 16^2/_3 \text{ lbs.}$$

300. Your cup runneth over.

301. The correct answer is 20. Don't forget that the number 33 has two threes.

302. Place "end" at the beginning of each word:

endear
endless
endanger

303. The answer is 3.

$$^3/_4 × \ ^1/_2 × 16 = \ ^{48}/_8 = 6$$
$$^1/_2 × 6 = 3; 6 - 3 = 3$$

304. It will take 63 moves. For any number of discs n, the number of moves can be found by $2^n - 1$.

305. Here's a list of 15 words. Are they anywhere near the words you came up with?

> serve
> vice
> rice
> ice
> see
> seer
> veer
> sieve
> eve
> rise
> ever
> sever
> cerise
> rive
> verse

306. The last number is 625. Subtract each individual digit in the numbers from 10 to crack the code.

307. A single discount of 12 percent is greater.

$$12\% \times 100 = 12.00$$
then
$$6\% \times 100 = 6.00$$
$$100 - 6 = 94$$
$$6\% \times 94 = 5.64$$
$$6.00 + 5.64 = 11.64$$

12.00 is greater than 11.64

308. Traffic congestion

309. The answer is zero!

310. YOU ARE A GENIUS. Move each of the letters in the puzzle back by three letters in the alphabet.

311. Draw a line from point 3 to point 12 and cut along the line to divide the figure. Turn the smaller figure upside down, then connect points 1 and 12 on the smaller figure with points 17 and 13, respectively, on the larger figure.

312. 8. The numbers represent the number of letters of each word in the question. "Sequence" has 8 letters.

313. An upward turn in the economy

314. False. Some pibs may be rews, but it is not definite.

315. The first calculation is $\frac{1}{3} \times \frac{1}{3}$ of 12×12, or $\frac{1}{9}$ of 144, which equals 16. The second calculation is $(12 \div 3 \div 2)^3$, or $(\frac{4}{2})^3$, or 2 cubed, which is 8. The correct answer is the first calculation.

316. Milepost 900. To solve this problem, recall that rate $\times$ time = distance. Let x be the time it takes the *Seneca Streamer* to reach the milepost. Then:

$$60 \text{ mph} \times (x + 3) = 75 \text{ mph} \times x$$
$$60x + 180 = 75x$$
$$15x = 180$$
$$x = 12 \text{ hrs.}$$
$$75 \times 12 = 900 \text{ mi.}$$

317. The cyclist can take 96 ($4 \times 8 \times 3$) different routes.

318. The correct answer is (d). To solve this, we need to find

$$\frac{3/7}{4/9}$$

Invert the denominator and multiply:

$$\frac{3}{7} \times \frac{9}{4} = \frac{27}{28}$$

319. Making up for lost time

320. Because there are two sides to the coin, the chances are always one in two.

321. Place a decimal point between the two numbers to get 4.5.

322. The weight should be placed five feet from the fulcrum. First, calculate foot-pounds on the left side:

$$(5 \times 10) + (6 \times 5) = 80 \text{ ft.-lbs.}$$

The right side must equal the left side:

$$16x = 80$$
$$x = 5$$

323.

P	= horizontal	△ △ △ △ = PAF
A	= triangle	MUFMAG = □
U	= square	□
G	= five	□
F	= four	□
M	= vertical	△
		△
		△
		△
		△

324. Overhead projector

325. It is 212 degrees Fahrenheit at which water boils.

326. The missing letter is S. Each letter is the first letter of the preceding number when spelled out.

327.

1. Unctuous — j. Oily
2. Riparian — b. Relating to the bank of a lake or river
3. Porcine — g. Relating to swine
4. Plexus — c. An interlacing network
5. Platitude — i. A trite remark
6. Cosmology — a. Study of the universe
7. Concatenation — h. A series connected by links
8. Alacrity — f. Briskness
9. Fecundate — e. Fertilize
10. Newel — d. An upright post

328. There must be at least 66 chocolates—the least common denominator for 3, 6, and 11.

329. E. There is one more circle and one less straight line inside each figure than the number of sides to the figure—except for figure E. This eight-sided figure is the odd one out, because it contains only six straight lines and only eight circles.

330. I returned on Tuesday. The day before tomorrow is today, Friday. The day after that is Saturday, and four days before Saturday is Tuesday.

331. I look up to you.

332. 15 hours. The problem can be solved as follows:

$$7,500 - 150x = 4,500 + 50x$$
$$3,000 = 200x$$
$$x = 15$$

333. He is 32 years old. Here's the formula for the solution:

$$x + 4 = (x - 14) \times 2$$
$$x + 4 = 2x - 28$$
$$x = 32$$

334. D is the only figure that doesn't have a straight line dividing it in half.

335. Multiple personalities

336. The probability is 1 in 132,600.

$$\frac{1}{52} \times \frac{1}{51} \times \frac{1}{50} = \frac{1}{132,600}$$

337. It weighs approximately 1,700 pounds! One cubic foot of water weights 62.4 pounds; one cubic yard (27 cubic feet) of water weights 1,684.8 pounds.

338. It must win 90 percent of the games. This is probably best expressed as follows: If a team wins 60 percent of one-third of the games, it is the same as winning 20 percent of all the games. Therefore,

$$20\% + \frac{2}{3}x = 80\%$$
$$\frac{2}{3}x = 60\%$$
$$2x = 180\%$$
$$x = 90\%$$

339. There are 50 stars on the United States flag.

340. It would be 4. The best way to solve this is by setting up proportions:

$$\frac{\frac{1}{2} \times 24}{8} = \frac{\frac{1}{3} \times 18}{x}$$

$$^{12}\!/_8 = {}^6\!/_x$$

$$12x = 48$$

$$x = 4$$

341. Here's one way to solve the puzzle

PART
WART
WANT
WANE
WINE

342. Upper crust

343. The answer is 1,234,321.

344. Growing concern

345. Six.

$$6m = b$$
$$8b = f$$
$$3f = y$$

We can find the number of bops in a yump by multiplying
8 × 3, or 24, and the number of murks in a yump by multiplying 24
times 6, or 144. So,

$$\frac{144 \text{ murks in a yump}}{24 \text{ bops in a yump}} = 6$$

346. The missing number is 448. In each triangle, multiply A times B and subtract 2 to get C.

347. It is 27 cubic yards—divide the number of cubic feet by 27 to get cubic yards.

348. A pear costs $.05. Here's one way to solve the problem. Letting p = pears and r = oranges, we have

$$(1) \quad 3p + 4r = 0.39$$
$$(2) \quad 4p + 3r = 0.38$$

Multiply equation (1) by 3 and equation (2) by –4:

$$9p + 12r = \quad 1.17$$
$$\underline{-16p - 12r = -1.52}$$
$$-7p = -0.35$$

Now we can solve for p:

$$-7p = \quad -.35$$
$$p = \quad .05$$

349. 227. In each column, divide the top number by 3 to get the bottom number. Then, add 3 to the sum of the top and bottom numbers to get the middle number.

350. $\frac{1}{2}$ or $-\frac{1}{2}$

$$\frac{1}{5}x \times 4 \times x = \frac{1}{5}$$
$$\frac{4x^2}{5} = \frac{1}{5}$$
$$4x^2 = 1$$
$$x^2 = \frac{1}{4}$$
$$x = \frac{1}{2} \text{ or } -\frac{1}{2}$$

351. Think of it this way: If the leader receives twice as much as each of the others, that's the same as having seven members all earning the same amount, which would be $175 each. If the leader earns twice as much, he or she would therefore receive $350 per gig.

352. Double play

353. The missing number is 3. The numbers correspond to letters on the telephone keypad or dial.

354. Close encounters of the third kind

355. You would say *birta farn*. Notice that the adjectives follow the nouns.

$$klar = \text{red}$$
$$fol = \text{shine}$$
$$birta = \text{apples}$$
$$pirt = \text{bicycles}$$
$$farn = \text{big}$$
$$obirts = \text{often}$$

356. The numbers are 61, 62, and 63. To solve this, let x be the first number; then $x + 1$ is the second number and $x + 2$ is the third number. An equation can be set up as follows:

$$x + (x + 2) = 124$$
$$2x + 2 = 124$$
$$2x = 122$$
$$x = 61$$

357. It equals 26. The midpoint between 20 and 32 is 26, and the midpoint between 16_a and 36_a is 26.

$$16_a = 20$$
$$\downarrow \qquad \downarrow$$
$$\text{Midpoint: } 26_a + 26$$
$$\uparrow \qquad \uparrow$$
$$36_a = 32$$

358. Over and over again

359. The word is "geometric."

360.

	1	
2	5	3
	4	

361. 80 people. When $^1/_4$ of the guests left, $^3/_4$ of the people remained. When $^2/_5$ of them left, $^3/_5$ of $^3/_4$ remained. When $^3/_4$ of the remaining people left, $^1/_4$ of $^3/_5$ of $^3/_4$ remained ($^9/_{80}$). Since 9 people were left at the end:

$$(^1/_4 \times {}^3/_5 \times {}^3/_4)x = 9$$
$$^9/_{80}x = 9$$
$$x = 9 \times {}^{80}/_9$$
$$x = 80$$

362. Blood is thicker than water.

363. 1,000—one thousand!

364. Stop in the name of love.

365. The probability is $(^1/_2)^5$, or 1 in 32.

366. If you hold any of these letters up to a mirror, it will appear exactly the same as on the page.

367. $^1/_3$. In this series you take $^1/_2$ of the previous number, then $^1/_3$, $^1/_4$, $^1/_5$, and finally $^1/_6$. One-sixth of 2 equals $^2/_6$, or $^1/_3$.

368. Statement (2) is true.

369. A bird in the hand is worth two in the bush.

370. Six is the maximum number of lines.

371. The missing number is 14 or 2. Pick any piece of the pie and look directly opposite that piece: the larger of the two numbers is 3 times the smaller number, minus 1.

372. The case costs $5; the binoculars cost $95. To solve this, let b = the binoculars and c = the case:

$$b + c = 100$$
$$b = 90 + c$$

Now substitute:

$$90 + c + c = 100$$
$$90 + 2c = 100$$
$$2c = 10$$
$$c = 5$$

373. Eight of the one-inch cubes have three blue sides—they were the corners of the four-inch cube.

374.
> FAST
> FIST
> MIST
> MINT
> MIND

375. It will take ten seconds. Because the first strike sounds at zero seconds, two strikes sound in one second, three strikes in two, etc.

376. Two eggs over easy

377. Sammy must be a girl.

378. I'd rather be in Philadelphia.
> — W. C. Fields

379. There are nine innings in a baseball game.

380. MAD

381. High hurdles

382. It might look something like this:
> 1, 2, 3, 4, 5, 6, 7, 8, 9, ✧, ☆, ✶, 10

(Almost any symbols could be used to represent the old numbers 10, 11, and 12.) Our old number 13 now becomes 10. If you choose to call this number 10, the new symbols would need new names, as would all the numbers that contain these two symbols.

383. There are 17 squares.

384. Frequency is measured in hertz.

385. Home stretch

386. Parliamentary

387. CMXLIV

388. The missing letter is R. Starting with the W in the first circle and moving counterclockwise in each successive circle, the words "What is the letter" are spelled out.

389. 2,047

390. The pursuit of happiness

391. Head

392. Arc de Triomphe

393. The second number in each box is the first number cubed plus three, so the missing number is 30.

394. Your odds are 2 to 3:

$$\text{Odds in favor of an event} = \frac{\text{Probability of favorable event}}{\text{Probability of unfavorable event}}$$

$$\frac{^2/_5}{^3/_5} = \frac{2}{3}$$

395. There are 42 triangles.

396. He went under the knife.

397. Bach. B-sharp and C are the same note.

398. 1–b, 2–e, 3–a, 4–c, 5–f, 6–g, 7–d

399. 3, 2. The numbers are arranged in alphabetical order.

400. Here are 15. Can you come up with more?

burn	numb
bun	sum
run	nub
sun	um
runs	men
rum	muse
use	ruse
user	

401. All worked up

402. H is the only figure that is pointing counterclockwise.

403. There are six points on the Star of David.

404. Be on time.

405. Z = −7

12		18		26		38		49
	6		8		12		11	
		2		4		−1		
			2		−5			
				−7				

The number in each row is found by subtracting the first of the two numbers above it from the second.

406.
　　　　　　　　　　FEAR
　　　　　　　　　　PEAR
　　　　　　　　　　PEER
　　　　　　　　　　PEEP
　　　　　　　　　　PREP

407. A diamond in the rough

408. Knocked for a loop

409. The answer is 72. The series goes like this:
$1^2 - 1, 2^2 + 2, 3^2 - 3, 4^2 + 4, 5^2 - 5, 6^2 + 6, 7^2 - 7, 8^2 + 8, 9^2 - 9$, etc.

410. There are 360 degrees in a square.

411. B and D are equivalent. "Fourteen yards square" describes a square measuring 14 yards by 14 yards, or 196 square yards.

412. Odds and ends

413. Celestial

414.
madam
level
civic
radar
repaper
deified
rotator
(and there are more)

415. You are the caddy, and your fee has probably just increased considerably.

416. Here's one way:

MEAL
MEAT
MOAT
BOAT
BOOT

417. Turn the other cheek.

418. It is 7:00 P.M.

Let x = the time it is now, and y = the time until midnight

$$x + 4 = 12 - y$$
and
$$x + 3 = 12 - 2y$$

Subtracting the second equation from the first, we get

$$1 = y$$
Then,
$$x + 4 = 11$$
$$x = 7$$

419. There are nine positions on a baseball team.

420. One possible answer: Shown below are the two original squares and a shaded square created by placing matchsticks 4 and 5 in the middle of each original square.

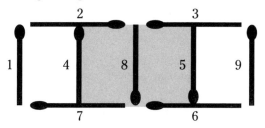

421. 8. Starting at both ends and working toward the middle, each pair of numbers adds up to 52.

422. The prefix is **sub-**.

423. Goldie is Nancy's aunt.

424. Pig Latin

425. If rounded up, the missing number is 6; if not, then the aswer is 5. The series (with a decimal point before the zero) represents the fraction $1/14$ expressed in decimal form.

426.
$$
\begin{array}{r}
9021 \\
581 \\
581 \\
581 \\
\hline
10764
\end{array}
$$

427. Three-point shot

428. Here's one way:

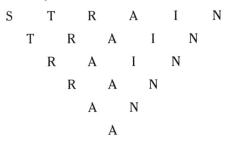

```
S    T    R    A    I    N
   T    R    A    I    N
   R    A    I    N
   R    A    N
      A    N
      A
```

429. 1 out of 2. There are 2^3 = 8 possible combinations when throwing a penny three times. Each combination has a $\frac{1}{8}$ probability, and four of them involve at least two heads:

HHH $\frac{1}{8}$
HTT
TTT
THH $\frac{1}{8}$
HHT $\frac{1}{8}$
HTH $\frac{1}{8}$
THT
TTH

430. 24

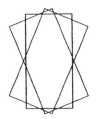

431. 50 and 40. Let x be the first number and y be the second number. From the statement of the problem we get:

$$x - y = 10 \ (1)$$
$$xy = 2{,}000 \ (2)$$

From Eq. (2) we get $x = \dfrac{2{,}000}{y}$. Substituting that value in Eq. (1) gives:

$$\frac{2{,}000}{y} - y = 10$$
$$2{,}000 - y^2 = 10y$$
$$-y^2 + 2{,}000 + 10y = 0$$
$$y^2 - 2{,}000 - 10y = 0$$
$$(y - 40) \times (y + 50) = 0$$

Therefore, we want the positive values for the above and they are 50 and 40.

432. Nobel Prize

433. 1,000,000 seconds is 11.57 days.

434. None. Instead, turn the puzzle upside down!

$$\begin{array}{r} 18 \\ 66 \\ +89 \\ \hline 173 \end{array}$$

435. PSV

436. BRAINTEASER

437. 1278. Each of the code numbers can be found by subtracting the original number from 2,000.

438. 1

$$84 \times {}^3\!/_7 = 36$$
$$36 \times {}^2\!/_9 = 8$$
$$8 \times {}^1\!/_4 = 2$$
$$2 \times {}^1\!/_2 = 1$$

439. $2^{(n+1)} - 2$

440. 61 and 91, respectively. Can you determine the pattern for any perfect cube, using integers only?

$$27 - 19 = 8 = 2^3$$
$$64 - 37 = 27 = 3^3$$
$$125 - x = 4^3$$
$$x = 125 - 64 = 61$$
$$216 - y = 5^3$$
$$y = 216 - 125 = 91$$

441.

The two figures in the first part of the analogy merge into one. When the squares merge, they turn into a circle. When the circles merge, they disappear. Circles and squares that don't merge stay as they are.

442. Too little, too late

443. $^4/_{10}$. This is actually two series within one: Starting with $^1/_7$ and looking at every other fraction, one series is $^1/_7$, $^2/_8$, $^3/_9$, $^4/_{10}$. The other series starts with $^4/_9$ and goes on to $^5/_{10}$ and $^6/_{11}$.

444. There are two pints in a quart.

445. Clams on the half-shell

446. Adam Mammale is not human.

447. Here's one way:

PARTY
PARTS
DARTS
DARES
DANES
DUNES

448. Lickety-split

449. The letters arrayed around the triangles spell out:

IT IS HIGH NOON

The number, therefore, is 12.

450. 15.12. Each successive number is found by taking the percentage of the previous number, starting with 100%, then 90%, 80%, 70%, etc.:

$$100 \times 100\% = 100$$
$$100 \times 90\% = 90$$
$$90 \times 80\% = 72$$
$$72 \times 70\% = 50.4$$
$$50.4 \times 60\% = 30.24$$
$$30.24 \times 50\% = 15.12$$

451. Here is one solution:

$$\frac{3}{6} = \frac{9}{18} = \frac{27}{54}$$

There is another solution. Can you find it?

452. A secret between friends

453. COMPLETED

454.

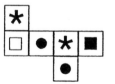

455. Prima donna

456. Quarterback

457. Either third or fourth

458. "Singin' in the Rain"

459. Stepbrothers

460. Cranberry.

461. Joseph could be my grandson.

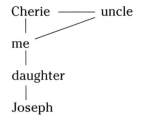

462. 55. Here is a proportion that solves this puzzle (where *x* is the unknown number of baseballs):

$$\frac{30}{9 \times 2} = \frac{x}{11 \times 3}$$

$$\frac{5}{3} = \frac{x}{33}$$

$$3x = 165$$

$$x = 55$$

463. B and D

464. We confess, we only found 44. Did you find more?

coin	fin	nice	one
con	fine	nine	scenic
cone	foe	no	scion
confess	I	noise	scone
confine	ice	none	sin
cosine	icon	noon	since
eon	if	noose	sine
fee	in	nose	some
fen	info	of	son
fess	is	on	sonic
fie	neon	once	soon

465. Pete has $^1/_{10}$ of the candy. Here's how to get the answer:
After Joe takes $^3/_5$ of the candy, $^2/_5$ of the bag is left. If Pete takes $^3/_4$ of the remainder, then Pete's share is $^1/_4$ of $^2/_5$, which is $^2/_{20}$ or $^1/_{10.}$

466. F = 23. Substituting Eq. (1) in Eq. (2), gives

$$A + B + P = T$$

And substituting Eq. (5) in this last equation gives

$$8 + B + P = T \qquad (6)$$

If we then substitute Eq. (3) in Eq. (4), we get

$$B + P + T + A = 30$$

Substituting Eq. (5) in this last equation gives

$$22 - B - P = T \qquad (7)$$

Adding Eqs. (6) and (7) gives the following:

$$8 + B + P = T$$
$$\underline{22 - B - P = T}$$
$$30 = 2T$$

$$\text{So, } T = 15 \qquad (8)$$

Substituting Eqs. (5) and (8) in Eq. (3) gives

$$F = 15 + 8 = 23$$

467. Ser

468. The order should be 4, 1, 3, 5, 2.

469. Here's one possible answer:

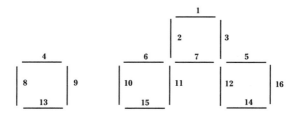

470. 168. The pattern behind this sequence can be revealed by factoring the individual terms:

$$5 = 2^2 + 1$$
$$8 = 3^2 - 1$$
$$26 = 5^2 + 1$$
$$48 = 7^2 - 1$$
$$122 = 11^2 + 1$$

This shows that the squares of the prime numbers are involved. So the next term in the sequence must be

$$13^2 = 168$$
$$169 - 1 = 168$$

471. 1) CAGI

2)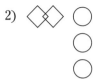

The breakdown of the relationships:

D = Horizontal
C = Vertical
A = ○
E = ◇
G = 3
B = 2
Y = Uncoupled
I = Coupled

472. Getting it all together

473. Bleary. Take the last three letters of each pair of words to form the new words.

474. MCDXLIX

475. It should be placed 16 ft. to the right of the fulcrum.

Left side: Currently there is a total of
20 ft. × 40 lb. + 10 ft. × 20 lb. = 800 + 200 = 1,000 ft.-lb.

Right side: Currently there is 10 ft. × 60 lb. = 600 ft.-lb.. Since this is less than what's on the left side, the 25-lb. weight must go somewhere on the right side. Let's call the exact distance from the fulcrum y:

$$10 \times 60 + 25y = 1,000$$
$$25y = 400$$
$$y = 400/25 = 16 \text{ ft.}$$

476. A bad spell of flu

477. $1\frac{1}{2}$

478. 21%. If you were to pick a student at random, the probability that he or she was taking at least one of the courses is 64% + 22% − 7% = 79%, which means there is a 21% chance that the student was taking neither course.

479. A = 1, B = 3, C = 2.

We can arrive at the answer via a plan of attack that examines the rules one at a time to chart the possibilities:

Rule (a): This raises two possibilities:

$$B = 2, A = 3, C = 1$$
$$\text{or}$$
$$B = 1, A = 3, C = 2$$

Let's assume one of these is correct and look at the next two rules.

Rule (b): This eliminates possibility (1).

Rule (c): This eliminates possibility (2). Therefore B cannot be equal to 1 or 2.

Rule (d): If B = 3, then A, not being 2, must be 1. And C, therefore, must be 2.

480. Here's one way:

> TIMER
> TIMES
> DIMES
> DINES
> DUNES
> DUNKS

481. "All Things Great and Small"

482. There are six outs in an inning.

483. The glass is $5/16$ empty. The $5/8$ is equal to $10/16$, which means that if the glass were $10/16$ full, you would have emptied $6/16$ of it. You empty $5/16$ of the glass first.

484. 125. 5 is 25 times $1/5$; likewise, 125 is 25 times 5.

485. British Open

486. D. Beginning with the S at the top of the first triangle and moving counterclockwise, the letters spell out STRETCH YOUR MIND.

487. Check-kiting

488. Eleven. Tom had to win four matches to draw even with Bill, and then Tom had to win three more times:

$$4 + 4 + 3 = 11$$

489. She is their aunt.

490. Ants in his pants

491. Here's one way to solve this:

$$^{8888}/_{88} - {}^8/_8 = 101 - 1 = 100$$

492. Here are three. Can you find more?

aardvark

mascara

anagram

493. "Star Wars"

494. 151. In each column, divide the top number by 3 to get the bottom number. Then add 3 to the sum of the top and bottom numbers to get the middle number.

495. Zero. The fisherman caught 3, 6, 9, and 12 fish on the second, third, fourth, and fifth days, respectively. If we let x represent the number of fish caught on the first day, then

$$x + (x + 3) + (x + 6) + (x + 9) + (x + 12) = 30$$
$$x + x + 3 + x + 6 + x + 9 + x + 12 = 30$$
$$5x + 30 = 30$$
$$5x = 0$$
$$x = 0$$

496. 86,400 seconds in a day

497. SCRABBLE

498. 24

499. 321. Divide 3 into 960 and add 1 (for the first term in the sequence).

500.

$$\begin{array}{r} 15 \\ \times 35 \\ \hline 75 \\ 45 \\ \hline 525 \end{array}$$

501. Pace back and forth.

502. The amateur's mother

503.

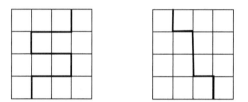

504. Because your chances of winning are 1 in 9. The probability of rolling a 2 is $^1/_{36}$; of a 3 is $^2/_{36}$; and of a 12 is $^1/_{36}$. And $^1/_{36} + ^2/_{36} + ^1/_{36} = ^4/_{36} = ^1/_9$. Thank your friend and buy him a drink.

505. 52%. First, we express the given fractions in terms of the least common denominator. Thus,

$$^1/_7 = {}^{11}/_{77} \text{ and } ^3/_{11} = {}^{21}/_{77}$$

Now we can restate the question as

"$^{11}/_{77}$ is what percent of $^{21}/_{77}$?"

This is the same as "11 is what percent of 21?"

And $^{11}/_{21} = 52\%$ (approximately).

506. Tocopherol is vitamin E. All the rest are minerals.

507. Reverse the charges.

508. $\dfrac{1}{2\sqrt{3}}$ or $\dfrac{\sqrt{3}}{6}$

Let the original fraction be $\dfrac{1}{x}$:

$$\frac{1}{x} \times \frac{4}{5} \times \frac{1}{x} = \frac{4}{5x^2}$$
$$\frac{4}{5x^2} = \frac{1}{15}$$
$$5x^2 = 60$$
$$x^2 = 12$$
$$x = \sqrt{12}$$
$$x = \sqrt{4 \times 3}$$
$$x = 2\sqrt{3}$$

Ans. $= \dfrac{1}{2\sqrt{3}}$ or $\dfrac{\sqrt{3}}{6}$

509. $26^2 = 676$
$101^2 = 10{,}201$

510. There were ten team members originally. Let x = the number of players and y = the price owed by each player, so:

$$xy = 50 \text{ and } (x - 2)(y + 1.25) = 50$$
$$xy = (x - 2)(y + 1.25)$$
$$xy = xy - 2y + 1.25x - 2.50$$
$$2y = 1.25x - 2.50$$

We know that $y = \dfrac{50}{x}$ so:

$$2\left(\frac{50}{x}\right) = 1.25x - 2.50$$
$$\frac{100}{x} = 1.25x - 2.50 \text{ or } \frac{100}{x} = \frac{5}{4}x - \frac{5}{2}$$
$$\frac{400}{x} = 5x - 10$$
$$400 = 5x^2 - 10x$$
$$5x^2 - 10x - 400 = 0 \text{ or } x^2 - 2x - 80 = 0$$
$$(x + 8)(x - 10) = 0$$

Only $x = 10$ will give a result of 0. So 10 is the number of original team members who ordered nachos for $5.00 each. When only 8 remained, they each owed $6.25, or $1.25 more apiece.

511. 30. Triangles ABC, ABE, ABH, ABI, ACD, ACE, ACH, ADH, AEF, AFG, AFH, AGH, AHI, BCD, BCH, BCI, BDH, BEH, BGH, CEF, CEH, CEJ, CFH, CFJ, CHI, DGH, EFH, EHJ, FHI, and FHJ.

512. The odd one out

513. 9,144. Break this sequence into different units and you will see the Fibonacci series;

$$1 - 1 - 2 - 3 - 5 - 8 - 13 - 21 - 34 - 34 - 55 - 8\underline{9 - 144}$$

514. $A = 1$ $B = 8$ $C = 9$
$D = 3$ $E = 4$ $F = 6$
Thus, $1 \times 8 \times 9 = 72 = 3 \times 4 \times 6$.

515. Here's one. Can you find others?

post
spot
tops
pots
opts

516. 30 beasts and 15 birds. Let b be the number of beasts and B be the number of birds. From the total number of feet, we know that

$B(2 \text{ feet/bird}) + b(4 \text{ feet/beast}) = 150$, or
$$2B + 4b = 150$$

The total number of creatures is $B + b = 45$,
so $B = 45 - b$

Now we can substitute this last equation into the feet equation:

$$2(45 - b) + 4b = 150$$
$$90 - 2b + 4b = 150$$
$$2b = 60$$

$b = 30$ beasts and $B = 45 - 30 = 15$ birds

517. $^1/_3$. The relationship between successive numbers, beginning with the first 240, is:

$1, ^1/_2, ^1/_3, ^1/_4, ^1/_5$ and $^1/_6$.
$^1/_6 \times 2 = ^1/_3$

518. 50. Compare the two equations as presented in this diagram:

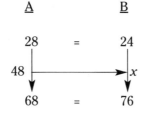

As you can see from the diagram, 48 is the midpoint between 28 and 68. We now need to find the midpoint between 24 and 76. We do this by adding 24 and 76, which equals 100, and dividing that by 2. Therefore, the answer is 50.

519. The word is PUZZLES. The answer can be obtained by putting each letter of the alphabet in a 5 × 5 grid, with *Y* and *Z* sharing the last box. The two-digit numbers are decoded by making the row number the tens digit and the column number the units digit of the letter being sought. Thus, for example, the code 41 represents row 4, column 1, which is the letter P. (*Note:* It was the ancient Greek historian Polybius who first proposed a similar method of substituting numbers for letters.)

	1	2	3	4	5
1	A	B	C	D	E
2	F	G	H	I	J
3	K	L	M	N	O
4	P	Q	R	S	T
5	U	V	W	X	Y/Z

520. 90°

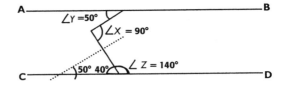

521. The figures correspond to each other as follows: A to E, B to F, C to G, and D to H. Blank squares in Figures A through D are filled with Xs in corresponding Figures E through H. Filled squares in Figures A through D are made blank. The correct figure is shown below.

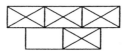

522. Each of the words can be made into at least two other words:

rifle: flier, lifer
evil: live, vile (and veil)
deal: lead, dale
rats: star, arts (and tars)
tale: late, teal

523. Only one doctor is a dermatologist. The other 99 are, of course, surgeons.

524. 76 trombones led the big parade

525. B

526. $93.26

$$
\begin{array}{r}
24.42 \\
54.42 \\
\underline{14.42} \\
93.26
\end{array}
$$

527. There are fifty-four external sides (the number of faces on nine cubes). Since two gallons are needed to paint one cube, you would need 2×9, or 18 gallons of paint to cover the figure.

528. 1. The first nine numbers of this sequence will repeat to infinity. They represent the consecutive integers from 1 to 9 squared with the resultant digits added together until a one-digit number is achieved:

$$1^2 = 1$$
$$2^2 = 4$$
$$3^2 = 9$$
$$4^2 = 16, \text{ and } 1 + 6 = 7$$
$$5^2 = 25, \text{ and } 2 + 5 = 7$$
$$6^2 = 36, \text{ and } 3 + 6 = 9$$
$$7^2 = 49, \text{ and } 4 + 9 = 13 \text{ and } 1 + 3 = 4$$
$$8^2 = 64, \text{ and } 6 + 4 = 10 \text{ and } 1 + 0 = 1$$
$$9^2 = 81, \text{ and } 8 + 1 = 9$$
$$10^2 = 100, \text{ and } 1 + 0 = 1$$

529. Line up in single file.

530. The value of R is 20. Because it is known that Q + M = C, it follows that Q + M + K = R. We also know that R + Q = S, so in the equation M + K + S = 40, we can replace S with R + Q. The equation then becomes M + K + R + Q = 40, or M + K + R = 32 because Q is 8. Rearranging the equations to solve for R, we then have:

$$8 + M + K = R$$
$$32 - M - K = R$$

$$40 = 2R \text{ and therefore } R = 20$$
$$\text{Because } R + Q = S$$
$$20 + 8 = S$$
$$S = 28$$

531. Tomorrow is another day.

532. $\dfrac{4!}{\sqrt{4}} = \dfrac{4 \times 3 \times 2 \times 1}{2} = 12$

533. The missing number is 259. Starting with 1, the sequence is as follows:

$$1^2, 2^2 + 1, 3^2 + 2, 4^2 + 3 \text{ (first circle)}$$
$$1^3, 2^3 + 1, 3^3 + 2, 4^3 + 3 \text{ (second circle)}$$
$$1^4, 2^4 + 1, 3^4 + 2, 4^4 + 3 \text{ (third circle)}$$

534. Crime wave

535. 1ΤΓ

These are the numbers 1, 3, 5, 7, 9, and 11, back to back with their reverse images.

536. $^1/_2$ lb. The $^1/_5$ lb. of chocolate is equivalent to $^2/_5$ of a block of chocolate. Multiply the $^1/_5$ lb. by $^5/_2$ to find the weight of the whole block:

$$^1/_5 \times {}^5/_2 = {}^5/_{10} = {}^1/_2 \text{ lb.}$$

537 Fight breaking out (or fighting across the border)

538. His wife bets the opposite of whatever her husband bets, usually double or triple the amount that he has placed.

539.

540. $\frac{2}{1}$.

These are the ratios of the frequencies of the eight notes of the diatonic scale, beginning with C. They are usually written

$$\frac{1}{1} : \frac{9}{8} : \frac{5}{4} : \frac{4}{3} : \text{ etc.}$$

541. LATITUDE

542. A piece of the pie

543. 5:00 A.M.

544. You bet it makes a difference! If $^1/_{30}$ were the true mean of $^1/_{40}$ and $^1/_{20}$, then neither dealer would have an advantage. However, the mean of $^1/_{40}$ and $^1/_{20}$ is 0.0375. The fraction $^1/_{30}$ is equivalent to 0.0333! So the buyers at the store across the street are being taken to the cleaners. The average of the reciprocals of two numbers is not the same as the reciprocal of the average.

545. 3 and then 2. The numbers are arranged in the alphabetical order of their spelled-out names.

546. D

547. BAR

548. There's a fine line between love and hate.

549. If you had three quarters, four dimes, and four pennies, which total $1.19, you couldn't make change for a dollar.

550. Name

551. No room for error

552. In 15 years. There are several ways to solve this puzzle, one of which uses a chart comparing their movements. It helps to realize that the correct answer must involve whole-number (not fractional) revolutions.

y (3 years)	x (5 years)
3 years = 1 revolution	$^3/_5$ revolution
6 years = 2 revolutions	$1^1/_5$ revolutions
9 years = 3 revolutions	$1^4/_5$ revolutions
12 years = 4 revolutions	$2^2/_5$ revolutions
15 years = 5 revolutions	3 revolutions

553. 7, 0. If you take the difference between each of the numbers, respecting whether that difference is positive or negative, you will find the following pattern:

$$3, 3, -7, 3, 3, -7, 3 \ldots$$

As you can see from this pattern, the next difference needs to be 3, which makes the first answer 7. The next difference is –7, which makes the second answer 0.

554. Separating the men from the boys

555. 24 miles per hour. Let's say Maria went 60 miles up and 60 miles back. It would then take her three hours up and two hours to get back. Five hours to go 120 miles is $^{120}/_5$ = 24 miles per hour.

556. 40. Here's one way to figure this out: there are 16 houses between number 12 and number 29. Since half of those have to be on each side, there are 8 more houses on each side. This makes the last home on one side house number 20, and there must be 20 more homes going back up the street, which makes a total of 40.

557. C. This is the only figure that has both concave and convex features. The other figures have one or the other only.

558. 45 miles. Let x be the distance from the beginning point to the turnaround point, and let y be the time it takes to go downstream. Then

Downstream: $\dfrac{x \text{ mi}}{30 \text{ mph}} = y$ (1)

Upstream: $\dfrac{x \text{ mi}}{10 \text{ mph}} = y + 3$

$$\frac{x}{10} - 3 = y \quad (2)$$

Setting Eq. (1) equal to Eq. (2) gives

$$\frac{x}{30} = \frac{x}{10} - 3$$

$$x = 3x - 90$$

$$2x = 90$$

$$x = 45 \text{ miles}$$

559. Alex is the second oldest. Their ages are: Alicia, 30 years old; Alex, 25 years old; and Amy, 5 years old.
Alicia, Alex, and Amy could also be 120, 100, and 20, but this is very unlikely.

560. TRIGONOMETRY

561. 7 in the second column, and 5 in the last column. If you delete the boxes and move the numbers together, you have a simple addition problem:

$$\begin{array}{r} 16367 \\ +27198 \\ \hline 43565 \end{array}$$

562. $1^7/_8$ hours. In one hour, the first pipe fills half the pool, the second pipe fills $^1/_5$, and the third pipe empties $^1/_6$. That is, in one hour the pool fills:

$$^1/_2 + {^1/_5} - {^1/_6} = {^{15}/_{30}} + {^6/_{30}} - {^5/_{30}}$$
$$= {^{16}/_{30}}$$
$$= {^8/_{15}}$$

For the whole pool to fill, then, it takes $^{15}/_8 = 1^7/_8$ hours.

563. Here are the ones we found. Did you find others?

math	thrice	timer	heat
rich	rice	crime	eat
chime	mice	crate	cheat
chimera	metric	cream	came
rat	time	ream	tame
cat	rime	treat	hater
hat	cite	threat	rate
mat	rite	tire	ate
tic	hate	mire	tea
mirth	mate	hire	team
chair	matte	it	mart
hair	act	teach	art
mare	tact	reach	cart
hare	them	meat	heart

564. There are five sides to a pentagon.

565. Counterculture revolution

566. Greater. Let x be the number of southpaws that are pitchers, y be the number of all southpaws, p be the number of all pitchers, and q be the number of all ballplayers. Then we have

$$\frac{x}{p} > \frac{y}{q} \text{ or } xq > yp \text{ or } \frac{x}{y} > \frac{p}{q}$$

567. –8. Above the line, either figure, circle or square, is worth +2 points apiece. Below the line, either figure is worth –2 points apiece. It makes no difference whether it is the circle or the square that comes first.

568. Standing at the end of the line

569. 6. Starting at the left, each group of three numbers adds up to 19.

570. Here is one way:

571. Root canal

572. Remove the vertical match in the plus sign and place it next to the match sticks at the beginning of the equation

$$(3 - 1 = 2)$$

573. Hg

574. 45. When $\frac{1}{3}$ left, $\frac{2}{3}$ of the people remained. When $\frac{2}{5}$ left, $\frac{3}{5}$ of $\frac{2}{3}$ remained. When $\frac{2}{3}$ of the remaining people left, $\frac{1}{3}$ of $\frac{3}{5}$ of $\frac{2}{3}$ (or $\frac{6}{45}$) of the people remained. Since there were 6 people remaining, there were originally 45 people.

575. FIRECRACKER

576. Tailgate party

577. Here's one way:
     TREAT
     TREAD
     BREAD
     BROAD
     BROOD
     BLOOD

578. Seven

579. Harvard would beat Montana by 16 points. Here's how to find the answer:

Maine beat BYU by 32 – 3 = 29 points, and Ohio State beat BYU by 10 – 7 = 3 points.

So if Maine were to play Ohio State, they would win by 29 – 3 = 26 points.

Notre Dame beat Ohio State by 14 – 10 = 4 points and, since Maine would beat Ohio State by 26, they would beat Notre Dame by 26 – 4 = 22 points.

Montana beat Notre Dame by 27 – 13 = 14 points and, since Maine would beat Notre Dame by 22, they would beat Montana by 22 – 14 = 8 points.

But Connecticut beat Maine by 28 – 24 = 4 points, so, because Maine would beat Montana by 8, Connecticut would beat Montana by 4 + 8 = 12 points.

New Hampshire beat Connecticut by 24 – 21 = 3, so, because Connecticut would beat Montana by 12, New Hampshire would beat Montana by 3 + 12 + 15 points.

Finally, Harvard beat New Hampshire by 1 point, so, because New Hampshire would beat Montana by 15, Harvard would beat Montana by 1 + 15 = 16 points.

580. 44

581. It's hip to be square.

582.

Daffodils	Smiths	1st Street
Roses	Johnsons	2nd Street
Violets	Parks	3rd Street
Begonias	Rosens	4th Street
Peonies	Morgans	5th Street

583. The missing number is 127. Starting with (7, 8), the difference between each enclosed pair of numbers is: $1^3, 2^3, 3^3, 4^3, 5^3, 6^3$.

$$6^3 = 216$$
$$343 - 216 = 127$$

584. Queen, queen, king, king, queen, king, queen, king

585. Male bonding

586. There are 14 days in a fortnight.

587. He who laughs last laughs best, or so they say.

588. Here's one solution:

> PEST
> PAST
> PASS
> BASS
> BATS

589. Same time next year

590. There are 31 bounded areas that are not further subdivided. One way to approach this puzzle is to look for a pattern: two circles have three bounded areas; three circles have seven; four circles have 13. Five circles would then have 21 bounded areas. The pattern is increasing 4, 6, 8, 10, 12 ... so six circles would have 21 + 10 or 31 bounded areas.

591. False. Some *zers* may be *wols*, but there is nothing to support the conclusion that some *zers* are definitely *wols*.

592. Here's one: POTPOURRI. What are some others?

593. A star in the making

594. It equals 25. Compare the two equations in the question:

The midpoint of column A is 24; the midpoint of column B is 25.

595. False. Even if the premise were true, it does not automatically follow that only the most brilliant minds will succeed. The conclusion is too open-ended. Who determines what represents brilliance? Is it simply a matter of intelligence tests, or are there other considerations? Who chooses the criteria? Who decides what success is? Many questions need to be answered before this argument can be considered valid.

596. PARALLEL

597. 13:71

Glass 1 is $\frac{1}{6}$ dye $+\frac{5}{6}$ water

Glass 2 is $\frac{1}{7}$ dye $+\frac{6}{7}$ water

Total dye in mixture =

$$\frac{1}{6}+\frac{1}{7}=\frac{13}{42}$$

Total water in mixture =

$$\frac{5}{6}+\frac{6}{7}=\frac{35}{42}+\frac{36}{42}=\frac{71}{42}$$

$\frac{13}{42}$ parts blue dye and $\frac{71}{42}$ parts water

598. Open forum

599. Figure 5 is the only one that doesn't include a square in its design.

600. Piece of cake

601. CALCULATOR

602. A friend in need is a friend indeed.

603. –9. The second number in each box is 1 less than the cube of the first number.

604. 7. The decimal representation of the fraction $^1/_{29}$ is .0344827. On some calculators, the digit 7 in that number is rounded off to 8.

605. 35. Bottom level, 18; second level, 12; third level, 4; top level, 1.

606.   Harry—June—Red
       John—Alice—Blue
       Brad—Nancy—White
       Steve—Sara—Yellow

607. A day at a time

608. There are 24 karats in pure gold.

609. Each is a different word when spelled backward. Such words are called recurrent palindromes.

610.

In each row, the pattern of lines in the second column has been subtracted from the pattern in the first column to produce the figure in the third column.

611. Meeting of the minds

612. I am 24 years old and my sister is 4 years old.
Here's one way to derive the answer. If my sister is x, I am $6x$. In one year I will be $6x + 1$ and she will be $x + 1$. Thus:
$$6x + 1 = 5(x + 1) = 5x + 5$$
$$6x - 5x = 5 - 1$$
$$x = 4$$
In six years, my sister will be ten and I will be thirty, or three times as old.

613. The words on the left have three consecutive letters of the alphabet in reverse order: <u>fed</u>eral, <u>pon</u>d, <u>rut</u>s. The words on the right have three consecutive letters of the alphabet in the correct order: <u>def</u>y, <u>hij</u>ack, ca<u>lmn</u>ess.

614. She put all nine scoops of ice cream into a blender and made milk shakes.

615.
$$982$$
$$982$$
$$982$$
$$+7982$$
$$10928$$

616. Spiral notebook

617. Here's how the words and the patterns are related: The letter L is used with the patterns whose individual components are separated. T goes with the patterns whose components are interlocked. R corresponds to three components and W to two. I goes with the snowman patterns, and U goes with the circles. For the two interlocked snowmen, the new word is TIW. The last pattern looks like this:

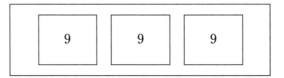

618. Pick up one penny on the first move and you can't be beat. Did you find any other winning move?

619. Border guards

620. Here's one way to solve the zookeeper's problem:

Put nine snakes in each of three cages, and put those three cages within a fourth, larger cage, in case any snakes escape from one of the smaller cages.

621. Twelve. Since 15 dealers have fewer than 5 cards, those 15 are eliminated from consideration. Three have more than 7 cards, so they are eliminated. Eleven have more than 6 cards, which means all 11 must have exactly 7 cards. This totals to 15 + 3 + 11 = 29 dealers, leaving one dealer we haven't mentioned (tricky, huh?), who must have exactly 5 or 6 cards.

622. 2,913. There are a couple of ways to solve this puzzle. The first way builds the series by summing squares and cubes in an interesting way:

$$
\begin{aligned}
1^2 + 2^3 &= 1 + 8 = 9 \\
3^2 + 4^3 &= 9 + 64 = 73 \\
5^2 + 6^3 &= 25 + 168 = 241 \\
7^2 + 8^3 &= 49 + 512 = 561 \\
9^2 + 10^3 &= 81 + 1{,}000 = 1{,}081 \\
11^2 + 12^3 &= 121 + 1{,}728 = 1{,}849 \\
13^2 + 14^3 &= 169 + 2{,}744 = 2{,}913
\end{aligned}
$$

Another approach involves taking the "difference of the differences." From the pattern continuing 48s that results, you can build back up the answer of 2,913:

```
9     73     241     561    1,081   1,849                     2,913
    64     168     320     520      768                    1,064
        104     152     200     248                    296
            48      48      48                      48
```

623. 225 squares on a Scrabble board

624. T, for thirteen. These are the first letters of the odd numbers, in ascending order, beginning with one.

625.   Here's a start:

raze	daze	red
race	read	dear
razed	dare	ace
raced	cared	aced
zed	care	are

626. *The Rise and Fall of the Roman Empire*

627. 1 mph. Bob was rowing at a constant rate, and it took him 8 hours to travel 24 miles. At the point where he lost his hat, he had been rowing for 6 miles, or 2 hours. To meet Bob where he began his journey, the hat had to travel downstream 6 miles. Bob didn't reach the hat until after he had rowed the remaining 18 miles, or for 6 more hours. Thus, it took the hat 6 hours to travel 6 miles, carried by the stream at a velocity of 1 mph.

$$6 \text{ miles}/6 \text{ hours} = 1 \text{ mph}$$

628. T. These are capital letters, beginning with A, that contain straight lines only.

629. 4

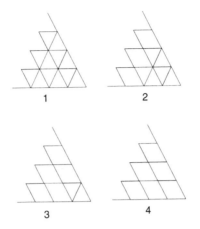

630. 90 seconds. In 1 minute the man can walk 1 length in the forward direction, but only one-third of a length in the backward direction. Factoring out the effects of the walkway's speed, we find that in 1 minute the man can walk

$$\frac{1 + \frac{1}{3}}{2}$$

or $\frac{2}{3}$ of a length in one minute. This means that the man can walk one length of the stationary walkway in $\frac{3}{2} \times 60 = 90$ seconds.

631. Chain link fencing

632. C. All of the patterns contain a figure similar to a capital F except pattern C, which has a backwards F.

633. FUTURISTIC

634. $(9!^{9!^{9!}})!$

635. Placed under arrest

636. You're as young as you feel. To decode, find the code letter in the bottom row and translate it into the corresponding letter in the top row:

A B C D E F G H I J K L M N O P Q R S T U V W X Y Z

L M N O P Q R S T U V W X Y Z A B C D E F G H I J K

637. 195. The lowest common denominator of 3, 5, and 13 is $3 \times 5 \times 13 = 195$.

638. Conundrum

639. Each is a 5-letter word that becomes a 4-letter word when its first letter is removed.

640. SYNONYM

641. 21. Starting with the two outside numbers and moving toward the middle, each pair adds up to 60.

642. Here's one version:

> PULL
> PILL
> PILE
> BILE
> BITE

643. Lowering the boom

644. 36. The sequence looks like this:

3	3	10	11	21	23	36
2(1) + 1	2(2) - 1	3(3) + 1	3(4) - 1	4(5) + 1	4(6) - 1	5(7) + 1

Index

Note: Answer page numbers are in italics.

Addition, 85 *(275)*, 134 *(297)*, 159 *(305)*

Age, 82 *(274)*, 103 *(283)*, 114 *(289)*, 127 *(294)*, 200 *(321)*, 220 *(327)*

Algebra, 10 *(233)*, 12 *(235)*, 18 *(242)*, 20 *(243)*, 30 *(248)*, 39 *(254)*, 45–46 *(257-259)*, 49 *(260– 261)*, 49 *(261)*, 53 *(262)*, 56 *(263)*, 58 *(264)*, 64–65 *(266)*, 68 *(268)*, 72 *(269)*, 73 *(269)*, 75 *(270–271)*, 76 *(271)*, 82 *(273–274)*, 83 *(274)*, 92 *(277)*, 98 *(280)*, 99 *(281)*, 107 *(285)*, 109 *(286)*, 112 *(288)*, 117 *(290)*, 120 *(291)*, 122 *(292)*, 124 *(293)*, 127 *(294)*, 131 *(295)*, 132 *(296)*, 133 *(296)*, 134 *(297)*, 136 *(298)*, 139 *(298)*, 170 *(308)*, 174 *(310)*, 180 *(312)*, 185 *(314)*, 187 *(315)*, 191 *(318)*, 200 *(321)*, 202 *(322)*

Alphametic puzzles, 9–10 *(232-233)*, 31–32 *(248)*, 104 *(283)*, 182 *(313)*, 190 *(317)*, 221 *(328)*

Anagram, 20 *(243)*

Analogies, 18 *(241)*, 22–25 *(244-245)*, 33 *(249)*, 80 *(272)*, 82 *(273)*, 105 *(284)*, 113 *(289)*, 146 *(300)*, 161 *(306)*, 177 *(311)*

Balance puzzles, 30 *(248)*, 72 *(269)*, 92 *(277)*, 98 *(280)*, 124 *(293)*, 174 *(310)*

Circles, 212 *(325)*. *See also* Letter wheels (circles); Number wheels (circles)

Clocks, 29 *(247)*, 111 *(287)*, 140 *(299)*

Code deciphering, 32 *(249)*, 119 *(291)*, 120 *(291)*, 160 *(305)*, 165 *(307)*, 188 *(316)*, 228 *(330)*. *See also* Cryptograms

Coin arrangements, 35–36 *(252)*, 40 *(254–255)*, 41–42 *(255)*

Cryptarighms. *See* Alphametic puzzles

Cryptograms, 14 *(237)*, 60 *(264)*, 81 *(273)*, 94 *(277)*, 141 *(299)*, 144 *(300)*, 168 *(307)*, 191 *(318)*

Cubes, 10–11 *(234)*, 20 *(243)*, 39 *(254)*, 42–43 *(256)*, 48 *(260)*, 71 *(268)*, 100 *(281)*, 132 *(295)*, 139 *(299)*, 161 *(306)*, 167 *(307)*, 170 *(308)*, 190 *(317)*, 196 *(320)*, 207 *(323)*, 208 *(324)*, 217 *(327)*

Division, 65 *(266)*, 66 *(267)*, 73 *(269)*, 109 *(286)*, 126 *(293)*, 174 *(310)*, 229 *(331)*

Drawing, 68 *(267)*, 194 *(319)*

Equations, 12 *(235)*, 171 *(309)*, 186 *(315)*, 187 *(316)*, 192 *(318)*, 201 *(322)*, 202 *(322)*, 213 *(325)*, 228 *(330)*

Exponential numbers, 14 *(237)*, 17 *(240)*, 37 *(253)*, 57 *(264)*, 62 *(265)*, 96 *(279)*, 100 *(281)*, 103 *(283)*, 109 *(286)*, 115 *(289)*, 189 *(317)*

Family relationships, 28 *(247)*, 89 *(276)*, 141 *(299)*, 155 *(303)*, 169 *(308)*, 178 *(312)*, 182 *(313)*, 197 *(320)*

Figure series, 47 *(259)*, 188 *(317)*, 193 *(319)*, 219 *(327)*

Figures that don't belong, 25 *(245)*, 47 *(259)*, 52 *(262)*, 66 *(267)*, 86 *(275)*, 126 *(294)*, 128 *(294)*, 148 *(301)*, 200 *(321)*, 215 *(326)*, 227 *(330)*

Foreign languages, 16 *(239)*, 90 *(276)*, 134 *(297)*

Fractions, 15 *(238)*, 50 *(261)*, 55 *(263)*, 56 *(263)*, 63 *(266)*, 67 *(267)*, 71 *(268)*, 71 *(269)*, 76 *(272)*, 77 *(272)*, 89 *(276)*, 92 *(277)*, 99 *(280–281)*, 111 *(287)*, 116 *(289)*, 118 *(290)*, 121 *(292)*, 129 *(295)*, 132 *(296)*, 136 *(298)*, 156 *(303)*, 160 *(305)*, 162 *(306)*, 165 *(307)*, 171 *(308)*, 174 *(310)*, 176 *(311)*, 183 *(313)*, 184 *(314)*, 189 *(317)*, 193 *(319)*, 194 *(319)*, 195 *(319)*, 205 *(323)*, 214 *(326)*, 230 *(331)*. *See also* Ratios

Frame games, 27 *(246)*, 33 *(249)*, 34 *(249)*, 44 *(256)*, 45 *(256)*, 50 *(261)*, 51 *(261)*, 52 *(262)*, 55 *(263)*, 56

(263), 58 (264), 59 (264), 60 (264),
61–62 (265), 64 (266), 66 (267), 67
(267), 69 (268), 70 (268), 72 (269),
73 (269), 74 (270), 75 (271), 77
(272), 78 (272), 79 (272), 80 (273),
81 (273), 83 (274), 84 (274), 85
(275), 87 (275), 88 (276), 89 (276),
91 (276), 93 (277), 95 (278), 97
(279), 98 (280), 100 (281), 101
(282), 102 (282), 104 (283), 105
(284), 107–108 (285), 110 (286), 112
(288), 114 (289), 115 (289), 116
(289), 117 (290), 119 (291), 121
(292), 123 (292), 125 (293), 127
(294), 128 (294), 130 (295), 131
(295), 133 (296), 134 (296), 135
(297), 136 (298), 137 (298), 138
(298), 140 (299), 142 (299), 143
(299), 145 (300), 146 (300), 148
(301), 149 (301), 150–151 (301), 152
(301), 154 (302), 156 (303), 157
(303), 159 (305), 162 (306), 163
(306), 164 (306), 166 (307), 167–168
(307), 169 (307), 173 (310), 174
(310), 176 (311), 177 (312), 178
(312), 179 (312), 180 (312), 182
(313), 184 (314), 186 (315), 191
(318), 192 (318), 193 (319), 195
(319), 197 (320), 198 (320), 199
(320), 202 (322), 203 (322), 204
(323), 206 (323), 208 (324), 210
(324), 211 (325), 213 (325), 214
(326), 215 (326), 216 (326), 218
(327), 220 (327), 222 (328), 223
(328), 225 (329), 227 (330), 228
(330), 230 (331)
Geometry, 21 (244), 28 (246–247), 52
(262), 53 (262), 63 (265), 107 (285),
139 (298), 158 (304), 188 (316). See
also Cubes; Triangles
Grid division, 183 (313)
Hidden phrase. See Frame game
Letters, 37 (252–253), 61 (265), 62
(265), 102 (282), 136 (298), 137
(298), 177 (312), 216 (326)
Letter series, 17 (240), 51 (262), 54
(263), 82 (274), 125 (293), 133
(296), 160 (305), 186 (315), 224
(329), 225 (330)

Letter wheels (circles), 29 (247), 84
(274), 144 (300)
Logic puzzles, 13 (236), 14 (237), 15
(238), 17 (240), 20 (244), 26
(245–246), 30 (248), 33 (249), 34
(250), 38 (253), 45 (256–257), 48
(260), 49 (261), 78 (272), 102 (282),
112 (288), 121 (292), 127 (294), 153
(302), 163 (306), 168 (307), 175
(311), 189 (317), 194 (319), 198
(320), 200 (321), 207 (324), 209
(324), 213 (326), 218 (327), 221
(327), 223 (328), 224 (328)
"Magic square," 68 (267)
Math, 21 (244), 78 (272), 118 (290),
123 (292), 144 (300), 158 (305), 178
(312)
Measurements, 143 (299), 152 (301)
Money, 49 (260–261), 68 (268), 197
(320)
Multiplication, 49 (261), 69 (268), 70
(268), 77 (272), 78 (272), 92 (277),
99 (280), 106 (284), 122 (292), 131
(295). See also Perfect numbers
Names, 45 (256–257), 47 (260), 57
(264), 83 (274)
Number grids, 68 (267), 101 (281),
109 (286), 111 (287), 132 (296), 180
(312), 201 (321)
Numbers, 35 (251), 60 (265), 65
(266), 71 (268), 79 (272), 109 (286),
117 (290), 134 (297), 136 (298), 149
(301), 179 (312)
Number series, 15 (238), 18 (240), 18
(241), 19 (242–243), 37 (253), 64
(266), 69 (268), 70 (268), 76 (272),
81 (273), 89 (276), 90 (276), 95
(278), 108 (286), 114 (289), 133
(296), 138 (298), 145 (300), 147
(300), 151 (301), 155 (303), 156
(303), 161 (305), 162 (306), 165
(307), 172 (309), 181 (313), 187
(315), 190 (318), 194 (319), 196
(320), 199 (320), 204 (323), 209
(324), 217 (327), 224 (329), 229
(331), 230 (331)
Number systems, 15 (238), 142 (299)
Number wheels (circles), 30 (247), 50
(261), 90 (276), 139 (298), 192 (318)

Odds. *See* Probability

Palindromes, 153 *(302)*, 185 *(314)*

Pattern formation, 15 *(238)*, 222 *(328)*. *See also* Figure series

Percents, 16 *(240)*, 58 *(264)*, 67 *(267)*, 85 *(275)*, 119 *(291)*, 129 *(294)*, 165 *(307)*, 175 *(311)*, 183 *(313)*

Perfect numbers, 80 *(273)*, 120 *(292)*

Periodic table, 205 *(323)*

Phrase completion. *See* Sentence/phrase completion

Probability, 13 *(236)*, 16 *(240)*, 32 *(249)*, 34 *(250)*, 39 *(254)*, 54 *(262)*, 74 *(270)*, 80 *(273)*, 88 *(276)*, 92 *(277)*, 116 *(290)*, 123 *(292)*, 128 *(294)*, 137 *(298)*, 145 *(300)*, 157 *(304)*, 183 *(313)*

Proportions. *See* Fractions; Ratios

Pyramids, 21 *(244)*, 96 *(279)*, 97 *(279)*

Ratios, 31 *(248)*, 59 *(264)*, 101 *(282)*, 103 *(283)*, 122 *(292)*. *See also* Fractions

Relationships, determining, 16 *(239)*, 110 *(286)*, 124 *(293)*, 169 *(308)*, 172 *(310)*, 173 *(310)*, 184 *(314)*, 189 *(317)*, 203 *(322)*, 217 *(326)*, 219 *(327)*, 229 *(331)*. *See also* Family relationships; Pattern formation

Revolutions, 28 *(246–247)*, 198 *(320)*

Roman numerals, 87 *(275)*, 108 *(285)*, 143 *(299)*, 173 *(310)*, 204 *(323)*

Sentence/phrase completion, 55 *(263)*, 63 *(265)*, 77 *(272)*, 86 *(275)*, 91 *(277)*, 96 *(278)*, 103 *(283)*, 125 *(293)*, 129 *(295)*, 141 *(299)*, 149 *(301)*, 151 *(301)*, 154 *(302)*, 162 *(306)*, 176 *(311)*, 181 *(312)*, 189 *(317)*, 202 *(322)*, 210 *(325)*, 219 *(327)*, 224 *(329)*

Series. *See* Figure series; Letter series; Number series

Speed, 28 *(247)*, 46 *(258)*, 53 *(262)*, 199 *(320)*, 225 *(329)*. *See also* Time-distance

Squares, 54 *(263)*, 56 *(263)*, 73 *(269)*, 76 *(271)*, 93 *(277)*, 96 *(279)*, 120 *(292)*, 135 *(297)*, 142 *(299)*, 155 *(303)*, 170 *(308)*, 172 *(309)*, 181 *(313)*, 204 *(323)*

Syllogisms, 14 *(237)*, 212 *(325)*

Time, 29 *(247)*, 127 *(294)*, 154 *(302)*, 159 *(305)*, 195 *(319)*. *See also* Clocks

Time-distance, 56 *(263)*, 109 *(286)*, 122 *(292)*, 200 *(321)*, 226 *(330)*. *See also* Speed

Triangles, 12 *(235)*, 44 *(256)*, 59 *(264)*, 115 *(289)*, 132 *(295)*, 138 *(298)*, 146 *(300)*, 185 *(315)*, 226 *(330)*

"Trickle-down" puzzles, 53 *(262)*, 74 *(270)*, 86 *(275)*, 94 *(278)*, 103 *(282)*, 113 *(289)*, 130 *(295)*, 140 *(299)*, 150 *(301)*, 153 *(302)*, 164 *(306)*, 175 *(311)*, 206 *(323)*, 211 *(325)*, 230 *(331)*

Unscramble puzzles, 20 *(243)*, 51 *(261)*, 63 *(265)*, 71 *(268)*, 88 *(275)*, 90 *(276)*, 95 *(278)*, 117 *(290)*, 143 *(299)*, 153 *(301)*, 160 *(305)*, 181 *(312)*, 194 *(319)*, 205 *(323)*, 210 *(325)*, 212 *(325)*, 214 *(326)*, 227 *(330)*, 229 *(331)*

Velocity. *See* Speed; Time-distance

Weight, 30 *(248)*, 49 *(261)*, 129 *(294)*, 193 *(319)*. *See also* Balance puzzles

Word chain, 157 *(304)*

Word match, 106 *(284)*, 126 *(293)*, 147 *(300)*

Words, 51 *(261)*, 65 *(266)*, 84 *(274)*, 94 *(278)*, 135 *(297)*, 166 *(307)*, 179 *(312)*, 187 *(315)*, 201 *(321)*, 212 *(325)*, 219 *(327)*, 220 *(327)*, 229 *(331)*. *See also* Sentence/phrase completion

Words, creating, 57 *(264)*, 60 *(265)*, 71 *(268)*, 79 *(272)*, 91 *(277)*, 99 *(280)*, 118 *(290)*, 118 *(291)*, 141 *(299)*, 144 *(300)*, 147 *(300)*, 155 *(303)*, 170 *(308)*, 171 *(309)*, 196 *(320)*, 201 *(322)*, 224 *(329)*. *See also* "Trickle-down" puzzles; Unscramble puzzles

WHAT IS MENSA?

Mensa®
The High IQ Society

Mensa is the international society for people with a high IQ. We have more than 100,000 members in over 40 countries worldwide.

The society's aims are:
- to identify and foster human intelligence for the benefit of humanity;
- to encourage research in the nature, characteristics, and uses of intelligence;
- to provide a stimulating intellectual and social environment for its members.

Anyone with an IQ score in the top two percent of the population is eligible to become a member of Mensa—are you the "one in 50" we've been looking for?

Mensa membership offers an excellent range of benefits:
- Networking and social activities nationally and around the world;
- Special Interest Groups (hundreds of chances to pursue your hobbies and interests—from art to zoology!);
- Monthly International Journal, national magazines, and regional newsletters;
- Local meetings—from game challenges to food and drink;
- National and international weekend gatherings and conferences;

- Intellectually stimulating lectures and seminars;
- Access to the worldwide SIGHT network for travelers and hosts.

For more information about Mensa International:
www.mensa.org
Mensa International
15 The Ivories
6–8 Northampton Street
Islington, London N1 2HY
United Kingdom

For more information about American Mensa:
www.us.mensa.org
Telephone: 1-800-66-MENSA
American Mensa Ltd.
1229 Corporate Drive West
Arlington, TX 76006-6103 USA

For more information about British Mensa (UK and Ireland):
www.mensa.org.uk
Telephone: +44 (0) 1902 772771
E-mail: enquiries@mensa.org.uk
British Mensa Ltd.
St. John's House
St. John's Square
Wolverhampton WV2 4AH
United Kingdom

For more information about Australian Mensa:
www.mensa.org.au
Telephone: +61 1902 260 594
E-mail: info@mensa.org.au
Australian Mensa Inc.
PO Box 212
Darlington WA 6070 Australia